A SECOND ACT IN LIFE

A SECOND ACT IN LIFE

Nick deSpoelberch

Copyrighted Material

A Second Act in Life

Copyright © 2023 by Nicholas deSpoelberch.
All Rights Reserved.

No part of this publication may be reproduced, stored in a retrieval system or transmitted, in any form or by any means—electronic, mechanical, photocopying, recording or otherwise—without prior written permission from the publisher, except for the inclusion of brief quotations in a review.

For information about this title or to order other books and/or electronic media, contact the publisher:

Nicholas deSpoelberch
stmichaelstands@outlook.com

ISBNs:
979-8-9872114-0-3 (hardcover)
979-8-9872114-1-0 (eBook)

Printed in the United States of America

Cover and Interior design: 1106 Design

To Erin, for never quitting on me.

*To Liam, Quinn, and Shay, for giving me
the three best reasons to never quit.*

*And to all those who taught me how
to walk this road to recovery.*

A SECOND ACT IN LIFE

*How we can all start over: A manual for
the defeated, the hopeless, the trapped.*

How a high school dean narrowly survives becoming another casualty of the opioid epidemic, restarts his life with a mission in counseling, and explains how anyone can create a second act in life.
—Nicholas deSpoelberch

TABLE OF CONTENTS

Introduction	xi
Act One—Falling Down	1
Act Two—Getting Up	29
Fear	51
The Voice	59
Mental Health	65
Neuroplasticity	73
Perception	79
Spirituality	91
Service	99
Conclusion	107

INTRODUCTION

"There will come a time when you believe everything will be finished. And that will be the beginning."
—Louis L'Amour

In May 2013 I sat sweating in my seat on stage amid the grandeur of St. Ignatius Loyola Church on Park Avenue in New York City's tony Upper East Side. Five hundred graduating seniors and their families filled the pews with the excitement and anticipation of completing Regis High School, a private Jesuit secondary school for Roman Catholic boys.

I had spent four years counseling and helping those young men get to this, their graduation day. I had earned the respect of the faculty and community through hard work and dedication. As dean of students, I'd assisted with their graduation rehearsal and had helped escort them into the church that morning.

However, despite this time of great celebration, I was sweating uncomfortably in my faculty gown. My body was quaking and jerking as much as my mind. I simply couldn't take it anymore. I didn't care about the graduation, the speeches, or the honors about to be awarded to wonderful young men I knew so intimately. This ceremony deserved to be the culmination of our pride as a community and mine as dean. Instead, it became the culmination of my destruction.

I stood up and walked off the stage, bypassing the altar and striding straight out the side door. Dumping my faculty gown in my office, I drove to a Walgreens parking lot in Norwalk, Connecticut, on a mission to meet a heroin dealer. Then, with thirty tiny folders of heroin in my hand, I made my way to a local beach, feverishly opening a few of the folders with one hand while trying to stay on the road with the other. So intense was my need to escape my emotional pain that every second I could save mattered. I parked at the beach on that warm July day, heated the chemical diacetyl morphine—otherwise known as heroin—in a large spoon, drew it up in the syringe, and injected that dirty brown poison into my veins.

Explaining how two very different people—the dean and the addict—came to exist within me is the purpose of this book. I will explain how I survived the part of me that wished me dead so that I could become a person who was once again granted my guiding spirit. Today, liberating others from the dark side of themselves is my greatest joy and utmost hope.

This book is written for those who have hit a wall in life, been hit by a wall, or cannot find their way around a wall. It is for the people who have crashed headlong into an arrest, a public embarrassment or career fiasco, a social disaster or marital explosion.

Many of us read the headlines about the destruction of others with morbid interest, but we rarely grant these souls the compassion they are owed or understand on a gut level what their experiences are like. This book is also for those whose "bottom" is mostly on the inside: people the outside world views as normal, but who, on the inside, are in agony and/or feel their lives are meaningless. Those who are desperate, hopeless, stuck. At some point, we've all had the experience of feeling trapped, whether it's in a marriage or relationship, in addiction, economic hardship, an unhappy or unfulfilling career, or confined by our own limited thinking and beliefs.

The mental health crisis fueled by the pandemic has clearly illustrated that a multitude of Americans feel trapped or hopeless in some aspect of their lives. This book is about and for those who hope a second act is possible, and it explains how to create that act. It shows one how to believe there can be a second, or a third, or a fourth act in life . . . to accept that change is possible and that a new act of life is waiting for you to show up and claim it.

We don't talk enough about our rock bottoms in life. People love to celebrate the apex of a person's redemption.

They eat up successful book and TV appearances, tabloid columns, and puff pieces emphasizing how low a person has fallen and how fulfilled they have become. We love celebrating someone who has risen high from debilitating lows.

But when they are still at rock bottom, we don't want to know them or be near them. Talking about and acknowledging the portion at the bottom of the "V" of people's personal disasters is rare and socially discouraged. No one wants to see or share those scandals and appalling actions, the complete demoralization that possesses us at the bottom of an addiction, a depression, or any other behavioral dysfunction.

If none of us tells that story, how do we expect our children and others to learn from us and be assisted in their own struggle? How can we expect people to not feel alone in their own lows? Without those lows there are no high points to celebrate. Don't live in shame of your low point. If you feel you have failed at college, a job or career, a marriage or relationship, you *can* decide to create something different.

We are all in the furnace of life, becoming *something*. When we become awake to a failure in what we are creating, we can amend and transform the process. We can adjust our energy and focus to radically correct the life we are producing. We must accept that destruction and that being shaped by life is part of the process. Your time in the trenches of your own suffering is the fuel you need to climb up that ladder and out of your misery. I write this from the perspective of having been a practicing mental health professional for twenty years, one who continues to recover from addiction, one who is crafting a second act I can be proud of living.

I am not a trained writer, and there are thousands of self-help books available. Yet I write this book with the belief that recognizing, developing, and sharing a meaningful message is achievable by anyone. That must include me, and it also includes YOU. Your words or actions of transformation are the only invitation someone out there will need to hear.

I also must give credit to the resources I consulted that inspired the beliefs and ideas contained in this work. The thoughts and philosophy laid down here are not original in any way. I am attempting to internalize and pass forward the wisdom I've encountered. The tradition of oral wisdom in recovery is a miracle, one evident in 12-step recovery programs. There was an original 12-step group in 1939 when *Alcoholics Anonymous* (also known as the *Big Book* in recovery circles) was published. Since that time, belief in recovery from addiction and a program to manage life's travails has been passed down from one recovering person to another. None of us invented it or can claim it as our own. Even the founding members of the first 12-step group, Alcoholics Anonymous, pointed to uncountable sources of spiritual, medical, and psychiatric influence in helping to create AA. Those roots have led all the way to my recovery, and I am both alive and useful as a result.

For twenty years I've counseled people who struggle daily. This has filled me with conviction in helping lost people in the search for their real selves. These include a homeless man with schizophrenia, a college student with debilitating depression, and a woman unfulfilled in her chosen career and buckling under the demands placed upon her, as well as a multitude of other people with poignant personal struggles.

What I see across many ages and demographics is the belief that a significant part of their life is a dead end—or they can't go on living their lives the same way. Many of us stay in our same rut for fear that anything different might be worse. Fear takes over, and we cling to a dead end out of familiarity, the belief that the suffering we know is better than letting go or that anything different is impossible.

In overcoming these problems, I will share the most valuable thing I possess: my story and my experience as a counselor. I'll explain how I came to my rock bottom in life and how multiple people, techniques, resources, and beliefs brought me back to a life worth living.

There are exercises throughout this book to encourage you to identify current obstacles and marshal your resources to act. We can restart and resurrect our life at any place and any time, so it becomes more beautiful than we imagined possible. The end of everything is the beginning of something.

What do you want to be free of at this time so you can start anew?

◆ ◆ ◆

FALLING DOWN

The end of my first act may admittedly be more dramatic than most. As a thirty-five-year-old dean of students at Regis High School, I seemed to be on top of the world. I was married with two young boys and had a prestigious job working with young people. Yet somehow, I was heavily addicted to heroin, alcohol, and benzodiazepines. I woke up each morning filled with terror and self-hatred. I didn't dare to look at myself in the mirror. This situation taught me well that the outsides of people's lives are not representative of their internal worlds.

I have struggled with generalized anxiety my entire life. I always felt that the volume of my anxiety was at an eight, while believing that most people lived with anxiety at a one or a two. Finding ways to numb or medicate that level of anxiety became paramount to believing I could function, particularly in social situations. I understand what it is like for people who never feel comfortable. It takes enormous energy to continuously think about others and their thoughts—so much that you fail to enjoy your own mental life.

From early childhood, I assumed that others spend more time thinking negatively about me than they actually do. There is a certain egotism to that, to thinking you are that important. It is pride in reverse. But it is nevertheless tortuous and unwanted, starting with the assumption that something is wrong with you or that people will have negative perceptions of you. Who could possibly ask for or desire such a thing? The moment you believe that, all social and interpersonal contact makes being around people hard work. It exacts a toll early on and is coupled with the false belief that most people have no such struggles. Yet for many people, social interactions do come naturally and fluently. Many report far less self-consciousness or preoccupation with others' mental conversations than do I.

For those who know this burden to any degree, I have a special empathy. It is living through fear and thinking too much about yourself to enjoy your life much. If we can never get more control of this feeling, our nerves remain under constant pressure, which undercuts all our relationships and activities. We fixate on others. "She definitely just rolled her eyes" ... "He just shunned me with his body language" ... "I can tell they don't like me."

Those with this insecurity can perceive disdain, dislike, or dismissal in every daily experience, where others would notice nothing negative. It often feels like living as an exposed nerve.

When you are around others with dark moods or extreme emotions, you feel as if electricity is being conducted through your nerves, taking over your body and mind. Whether a disgruntled person directs anger at you, or a friend suffers a tragic loss, their state can temporarily override your logic and reason and "gives you" their feeling. Clearly, it is profoundly important for human beings to possess empathy. But there remains a distinction between feeling what others are feeling versus feeling flooded, imbalanced, overtaken by their feelings. You become a tail wagged by every extreme emotion you experience.

Healthy empathy implies a separation between others' emotional states and retaining control over your own. Remaining unaware of and unable to separate from others' feelings results in emotional torture. You find yourself living in other people's moods and minds as much as you live in your own. Scores of people wrestle with this curse. We seek relief from it in all manner of chemical interventions and behaviors. There is no landlord stingier than fear.

For me, this unhealthy state of mind was impacted by where I grew up. In Fairfield County, Connecticut, I was surrounded by massive wealth, prestige, and expectation. I felt chronically uncomfortable in the preppy culture that dominated most of my early life. Although I was lucky to grow up with ample food and clothing and in comfortable surroundings, I felt the vibe given off by many neighbors and friends translated into: "We are the highest form of people, the pinnacle of humanity."

Some of this belief can be attributed to my never feeling confident, to sensing that I was not that great a person. Cockiness and entitlement were the opposite of how I felt. I don't intend to malign Fairfield because there are also wonderfully charitable and humble people living there. Yet my perception was that people had a lot of money and possessions—but little real meaning and purpose in their lives. It was a stark disparity.

Additionally, from the age of eight, when my father's alcoholism became severe, fear formed the background of my life. His alcoholism played a huge role in my development. My father was a Dr. Jekyll and Mr. Hyde drinker. Sober, he was reserved and generally easygoing. But put some vodka in him and his rage flowed out, onto me and my mother. Anger at his dissatisfaction with different areas of his life and perceived disrespect crashed down on anyone close by.

When my father was two, his father was killed test-piloting a plane for the Belgian Air Force. His mother struggled with the loss of her husband and the family's arduous flight from Europe during World War II. She became incredibly overbearing and intense, fueling the anxiety he struggled with and compounding the pressure he felt. His older brother excelled at Harvard and had a prestigious career working with the UN all over the world. My uncle always seemed like an impossible sibling to catch up to. The combination of stress and pressure created the susceptibility for alcohol to control my dad.

One day, I was lying on a kitchen table with my feet dangling off it. I felt his fists close around my ankles and a violent jerking motion. The sensation of falling was followed by my skull hitting the tile floor. I remember pain and confusion, followed by the muffled sounds of my mother yelling. When my father's drinking ramped up, my fear grew, and with it came a new friend: anger/rage.

It can actually feel intoxicating and refreshing when you have been terrorized by fear. I stood up to my father several times in defense of my mother when I was eleven years old—and paid the price. He usually threw me on the bed or pushed me away, and I was too small to be a threat. I felt powerless, knowing it was right to defend my mother but not having the ability to do so. I would throw everything in my heart and body into the attack and be swatted away like a gnat. One day, I snapped at my father in front of three of my twelve-year-old friends. He grabbed my arm and twisted it behind my back, cranking my wrist to inflict pain as my horrified friends gaped.

As I rounded the corner on my twelfth birthday, that combination of fear and anger was the perfect mixture to produce drug-seeking and self-medicating behavior. From that beginning, alcohol and marijuana seemed the answer to my problems. Fear disappeared, and for quite some time it was easily blocked with either substance. Alcohol and marijuana often muted the self-consciousness that was so paralyzing and draining.

Those in recovery frequently reminisce about their first feelings of full comfort in social settings. Why? Because being set free from crippling self-consciousness is astonishingly liberating for those whose mental environments have been chronically unpleasant. This comfort feels like floating peacefully in the water after a life of struggling underwater and fighting to reach the air. It is no wonder that with these transformations from tension to ease, so many of us struggle to accept that drugs and alcohol can no longer grant us that relief.

Sadly, drug-and-alcohol infused moments produce such a powerful punch of euphoria that the brain captures them as cherished memories to refer to in moments of tension or struggle. Those moments become seemingly matchless experiences of what life *should* feel like. In comparison, anything else feels insufficient. Twenty years after my first drug experiences, my brain was still pointing arrows back to those times of perceived freedom, especially when I felt stressed or bored.

Since chemicals offered those feelings, little wonder that I could never use them in moderation. Between ages twelve and sixteen my drug use overtook every part of my life and tolerance to these substances grew. Sadly, they had less effect over time, and fear and depression still found their way to me.

Being chemically dependent makes sober moments even more uncomfortable, resulting in more anger and active resistance to parents and authority figures. My deep dive into substances lasted until I was sixteen. One night, I was trying to shut off a nine-hour hallucinogenic trip on psylocibin when I observed two large human outlines at the foot of my bed.

These were towering professional escorts my parents contracted who woke me up and gave me a simple choice:

comply with us or be handcuffed as we deliver you to a residential program. This was a terrifying experience, even without a psychedelic trip. I sweated and endured thirty days in the middle of the Idaho desert to detox before being delivered to a therapeutic boarding school in Massachusetts. I spent my sophomore to senior high school years at the John Dewey Academy. At the time, many therapeutic boarding schools were guided by the Daytop Village philosophy of tough love confrontational therapies and intense community life.

Daytop Village was a substance use program started in 1963 in the Bronx, New York, and modeled on a therapeutic community called Synanon. The principle that people must be broken down psychologically in order to be rebuilt was powerful back then and popularized through books, articles, and experts. Although mainly abandoned by the larger therapeutic industry today, this philosophy produced significant controversy and widespread reports of physical and emotional abuse at facilities that practiced it.

The model focuses on peer interactions, confrontation groups, and a hierarchy, with newer members having no privileges. Eventually, I found this community to be a place where I could belong and flourish. However, the idea that a person can and should be changed via brute force, group attacks, and public shaming is misguided and frequently leads to abuse. Early in treatment, troubled youth are elevated to positions of status and power over newer members, and unhealthy boundaries inevitably result.

Among many of the most severe interventions was "sitting the chair." Moved to a chair on an auditorium stage, one passed days on display to the community as result of breaking norms and falling into disfavor. That was the confusing part about the school. If the students or staff with influence decided they didn't like you or you were harmful to the community, they could find ways to drive you out of the school or at least make things harder. When sitting the chair you slept and spent every minute, besides bathroom breaks, sitting, writing, and contemplating your transgressions and your desire to rejoin the community. Suffice it to say, being shamed for days on end was the opposite of attending high school proms and Pep rallies.

Sobriety returned me to the self-consciousness and expectations of judgment I knew from childhood. It caused me to work tirelessly to fit in and be deemed a good example to adults and students. There were good outcomes from this, but in retrospect I was still dominated by worries of others' perceptions. I can't quite call mine a peaceful mind, but the experience stabilized me enough for a few years to graduate high school and make some close friends for the first time.

Being immersed in a community of people who experienced anxiety and mental health issues also allowed me to feel less alone. Upon my graduation in 1997, the boarding school created the Nicholas deSpoelberch Award, presented to one student a decade who most upholds the school's values. The award symbolized the best part of me. It represented the spirit that had been awakened in me by being forced into a sober environment with a focus on honesty and spirituality.

It gave me a love for serving others that has been my salvation ever since. That salvation arises only in the presence of sobriety and spirituality. Without both, spirituality is lost to its opposite—the selfishness of addiction.

With time free from chemicals and feelings of peace from healthier actions, I found my spirit emerge for the first time. I was able to meditate, pray, and feel a connection to spirituality. An example of this was expressed in a scene from the admittedly cheesy movie *Braveheart*. The king is advising his son that he must betray the revolutionary leader William Wallace to the British nobles in order to protect their power.

> Robert La Bruce's father: "All men betray. All lose heart."
>
> Robert La Bruce: "I don't want to lose heart! I want to believe, as he does. I will never be on the wrong side again."

This scene awakened passion in me because I had lost heart in my life through depression magnified by drug use. I was in an intensive therapeutic environment, still in shock from my forced removal from home, the severing of all my social supports, and a father who had just gotten sober and whom I still hated. I realized how much I wanted that which chemicals had blocked me from attaining.

The movie scene was an important reminder for me that I did want to believe in something... that I needed to believe in something to transform my personality ... that life without belief is like a sail without wind. I have learned only in retrospect how much those emotional beacons matter. Whether they seem cheesy or not, they are evidence of the presence of our spirit and the urgency to listen to the things that call to it. When we don't listen or we allow people to dismiss our feelings, we resume our singular focus on the physical world and stop hearing the spirit.

When I started Sarah Lawrence College that fall, I was planning to remain sober and major in poetry. Ironically, I would have become a far better poet had I remained sober. Remaining sober for the first two years of college was challenging but rewarding. But my difficulty in socializing and being hypersensitive to others' reactions created a level of tension I could tolerate for only so long.

Deciding to break my abstinence at the beginning of my junior year was disastrous, but it felt unavoidable. The increase in my internal mental chatter and self-consciousness drowned out the spirit of freedom I had felt. We can cope with social discomfort and mental strain for only so long before pursuing relief in some form. I consistently chose the wrong form.

Had I immersed myself in prayer, met with a priest, attended meditation classes at a local Buddhist temple, or even confided in close friends about my struggles, this would likely be a very different story. Once again, alcohol, marijuana, and cocaine took over my life. For those of us with chemical dependence issues, we must admit there is no controlling the faucet of a chemical in our life. It's either on or off. Control is an illusion.

I graduated two years later, barely. As usual, the presence of addictive chemicals dulled my internal pain but created myriad problems, including a scrambled brain unable to retain or sincerely engage in the academics for which I was in college. Alcohol propelled me into constant socializing and parties with temporary pleasures.

Other people who attended those parties had a life distinct from the parties. I drank, regardless of any social events, because it was just about the drinking. That is alcoholism. "The man takes a drink. The drink takes a drink. The drink takes the man." It is the saddest thing I know to remember the extent to which I didn't drink the alcohol—the alcohol drank me. It drained the good I did have to offer, blocked me from maintaining any deep relationships, and created a life of subordination to the chemical.

Following college, I sought a way out of my pain and dysfunction. Committing to finding myself through helping others, I got a job as a mental health worker at Four Winds Psychiatric Hospital in Katonah, New York. For five years I worked in this inpatient psychiatric hospital, attempting to provide some relief to adolescents and find more peace within myself. Watching people in pain is both troubling and inspiring. A river of pain flows through this world. Being in a psychiatric unit, I was knee-deep in it. The cases of psychotic, suicidal, anxious, depressed, oppositional young men and woman affected my spirit in both beneficial and harmful ways.

Counseling those who seemed without hope, I also witnessed unparalleled strength and grace. It is beautiful when people find help in treatment or come to believe in themselves and their ability to transcend their problems. I struggled at times to fit into the tightknit staff community, especially seeing that some staff members appeared to have disdain or disregard for patients.

I am never surprised to learn of someone experiencing mental suffering. When people belittle others' suffering and mental anguish it disgusts me. Patients' behavior can sometimes be obnoxious, violent, and unacceptable, but treating them with ridicule and disdain only makes a dark situation darker. It's impossible for me to not feel others' pain. That absolutely can be a liability when it prevents you from drawing appropriate boundaries.

If we are too understanding, we can fail to confront others on inappropriate behaviors. I learned a lot about service when I stood among the suffering and offered some kindness, listened carefully to their anguished thoughts, and helped them resolve suicidal ideations and gather the hope to go back into the world. It is this experience that led me to attain a master's degree in counseling and, at that time, to become a school counselor.

The offer of a job at Regis High School in 2006 was something I could not turn down. This prestigious Jesuit high school boasts a brilliant student body and remarkable academic reputation. It was founded in 1914 for Catholic young men with high leadership potential and intelligence. A Jesuit foundress started it to ensure that bright young Catholic men from any economic background could attend a great institution and flourish in the world. It corresponded well with my desire to work somewhere with a mission of service.

As a guidance counselor at Regis for the next three years, I was fortunate to counsel hundreds of young men. Many came from poor or modest backgrounds and displayed remarkable humility and gratitude for the gift of an excellent education. Their intelligence was astounding, but their anxieties and immaturities were identical to those of other adolescents.

I loved the job. The individual counseling filled me with great passion and satisfaction. I felt useful to the world and at relative peace.

A little background on my alcoholism until this point. On my first date with my future wife I rushed a shot of Jager hard liquor while she was in the bathroom. It was simply anxiety management over a woman I really liked and a date I wanted to go well. I don't know why, but I tried to convey that to her. She took it as an alarm bell and confronted me about it. Then, months into our relationship, she discovered I was adding water to her Scotch bottle to disguise the amount I ingested. Feeling I must hide the amount I consumed of a drug or alcohol was a terrible omen of things to come. After we were married my wife was very alarmed, but I was consistently able to turn down or turn off the drinking when her attention was on it. During the marriage, I became a binge alcoholic. I had periods of abstinence and successful limits on my drinking. I also had physical fights, fell down the stairs, and had two DUI charges. Twice in my life I was hospitalized because I drank to the point of blackout and lashed out at groups of men that I thought were being disrespectful to me. They beat me viciously. Both times, it took weeks for my face to resume the shape I recognized. When that much alcohol was in me, it brought me face-to-face with my father's actions and the same desperate rage at the world. My wife was an innocent bystander to the disease that was unfolding inside me. She did everything a person can do to save me from it, and if love was a cure for alcoholism, I would be long healed.

By 2008 I had fulfilling counseling years behind me and two years of abstinence from alcohol. This was a result of the relative balance and psychological comfort emerging in my life. With my marriage, a child on the way, and my service to the school community, I felt less mental static and anxiety than ever. I felt both loved and useful. I knew my spirit to be inside me and felt its power.

When I was offered the role of dean of students in 2008, I had some hesitation, but the salary increase seemed necessary to support my wife and growing family. I rationalized that "this is just what people do." If I could go back in time, I would advise myself and you that "this doesn't mean it's the right thing for YOU to do."

Many of us make similar choices that create a trap for ourselves down the road, placing us in direct conflict with our values or abilities: picking the wrong spouse, choosing a job or career we know is not ideal, making a likely well-intentioned but uninformed choice about what is best for us spiritually and mentally. Choosing what is best for short-term happiness or material gain can bookend the first act of our lives, ensuring that an obstacle is ahead that must be addressed.

Many times, I have witnessed the great suffering a person undergoes when trying to metaphorically jam a round object into a square hole—trying to force reality to conform to them through sheer will. In other words, trying to control others by twisting them into what you need them to be . . . trying to capture material gains at the expense of spiritual peace. Whether grinding ourselves down in a failed marriage or slaving at a career we "can't afford" to quit, we humans have a miraculous ability to drain our life force away in jobs we don't want and with people who no longer give us anything of value.

Although not everyone has the luxury to walk away from a job or marriage easily, I believe it's imperative to help people gain courage and be willing to take risks when present circumstances are unfulfilling. The alternative is accepting your misery is permanent and occupying the role of victim.

I served as dean of students for five years. The increased need to speak to large groups, to be a public part of the administration, and to hold students accountable for their behavior by enforcing consequences put me outside of my comfort zone and exacted a toll. I depended more heavily on the use of the benzodiazepine medication Xanax to cope with the sudden wave of higher responsibility and pressure that came with the job.

It is one thing to work with a student as a counselor. It is another to possess significant power, confront students over their behavior, enforce school policy including suspension/expulsion, monitor the safety of the population, and answer to faculty and parents about school policies. I often felt I'd gone from friend to cop, from compassionate advisor to cold arbiter of justice. It was a jarring switch.

You shouldn't take a job like that if you cannot bear knowing that even one other person doesn't like you or approve of your decisions. It didn't matter if 539 students liked me. If I knew that the 540th was talking trash about me giving him detention, I couldn't let it go. Handing out often serious judgments that control students' time and imposing penalties can guarantee resistance and resentment. To know of and hear peoples' resentments about you on a regular basis is a normal day for a dean of students, but for me it became intolerable.

I needed to be seen as fair and compassionate. This was difficult to explain to others and still seems ludicrous to me. When students would make massive mistakes, I couldn't help but feel compassion for them and did my best to both enforce a fair consequence and help them take a lesson from it.

Feedback then and since has validated that I accomplished enough that I should have felt content. At the time, though, work felt like living in a barbed wire suit. For three years I gave everything I had as my energy level wore down. The discomfort of always feeling "on the job" aided the deterioration and upped my dependence on benzodiazepines and opioid medications. I committed more of my time and energy to the school than was available to me. Emails and calls were constant, and I take responsibility for feeling I had to read every one and worrying excessively about my response or tone.

Many of us have experienced the phenomena of 24-hour-a-day work responsibility. That need to be accessible can be disastrous. There is no barrier between our personal life and work, no ability to release the tension accumulated between 9 and 5. How much mental health damage is created by the expectation of constant accessibility? At the end of the day, we are responsible for choosing such a job and signaling to employers that we are always available. At the same time, realize that people will keep pushing you as long as you keep saying yes. You must learn your boundaries and what you can tolerate.

Not only was the pressure too much for me, but Xanax as a sedative was no longer sufficient. Oxycodone and Vicodin became my drugs of choice. Yet I was proud that despite my addiction to opiates I'd never turned to street dealers to supply them. We addicts all have our strange pride of what makes us less bad than others, and that was mine.

A large part of the illusion I wove through my life is that every opioid I ingested was legally prescribed. That this was "responsible" medication. That illusion eventually swallowed the truth: I was consuming one-month supplies of oxycodone in four to five days and lying about another "lost prescription" for a second refill. When a doctor decided I had "lost" too many prescriptions, I adeptly located yet another pain management specialist in Manhattan (of which there are many), spun my exaggerated tale of severe back pain, and walked away with another script signed off on by an MD.

The psychological pain of that double life and the physical cravings and withdrawal that become constant companions forced me on a hellish rollercoaster loop. For many, such a loop increases in speed and force until death, intervention, or a miracle.

The crucial lesson I take from this time is that I allowed the belief that I was trapped in my job to take root and grow. I decided I was powerless to make any change. When you do that, you turn out your inner lights. I had a second young son on the way and a stay-at-home wife. They depended on a good salary coming in to support them. Taking a different counseling job would have meant a much lower, insufficient salary. I rationalized that one should suck it up and suffer. That's what men do. I don't know where that belief comes from, but it is deadly.

I believe most of us live in traps of our own making. When we decide we have no choice, bars as real as steel encircle us. We feel helpless and believe we need to just get through it.

The light in my soul started to dim on my long commutes into the city: shuffling onto packed trains in the cold mornings with a frantic mind, then returning home on dark trains, nervous with worry about the constant stream of work tasks. During the last years of my active addiction, 2012–2013, my soul hurt. It ached in despair; I had a deep longing for an end of some kind, be it death or overdose.

It is hard to describe how disappointing it was to wake up. To still "be" each morning was terrifying.

Every day's first thought is of supply. To rush to the bag or drawer to check on pill or powder or alcohol supply. Realizing that you have enough to make it through another day in your life is paramount.

The Latin root of the word addiction, *addicere*, is "to be enslaved to." The heavily addicted individual is in a trap of his or her own creation.

Of course, the chemicals themselves play a powerful role in shaping and controlling our need to prioritize their use over all else in life. Yet we are eventually forced to admit that "I did this" and have lost all control.

I lived as a zombie that last year: wake up, use heroin, go to work in depression and darkness, use heroin, hide out, seek as little contact as possible with people, return home, use heroin, and be a million miles away from an emotional connection with my family.

I switched my commute from train to car to isolate even further from humanity and not feel self-conscious digging for pills around "normal" people. I had been nervously digging for pills for years in the middle of packed trains and was often sure people *knew* what I was doing. The last six months of my addiction I slammed into at least four cars on the drive to Manhattan and bumped into dozens. Twice, the victim saw me and took off. No demands for insurance or apology, just the decision that getting away from me was the best option. Climbing in my car at 5 p.m. I began drinking the warm vodka under my seat, took more of whatever pills I had, and drifted home in gridlock and despair.

And why? Because I had decided I was trapped? I can admit now that I built the cage, designed the walls, and decorated every inch of my prison. My feeling of being trapped came about through a high level of despair and spiritual suffering, and it was as real as any cell.

Opiates are a cruel drug. They take away our fear, doubts, and anxiety all too well. What you learn only after you have become dependent on drugs is that they are also taking away everything good. Humor, joy, awe, wonder—we cannot access these feelings while wrapped in a narcotic blanket, yet we are forced to keep ingesting the poison that makes us hate ourselves. The mind forgets how to experience comfort without the chemical.

I heard someone say, "I didn't go to the bar and order a round of self-loathing or crush up a bag of shame and snort lines of it, but that is what I got."

Somewhere along this journey the soul dies. This cannot be described well in words but is very real. This is an overwhelming feeling that affects people facing all manner of obstacles. We know at some level when the soul or spirit is being damaged or ignored by our life circumstances. People play mental games with themselves. We find numerous rationalizations to defend why that damage or neglect is necessary or acceptable. But how much damage do we/can we accept before we resign and sign off on our own personal degradation or destruction in a career, relationship, or an addiction? Unsurprisingly, we often become stuck at a dead end and passively accept our fate, losing the energy we once had to act on our convictions and find a new direction in life.

Our rationalization to stay stuck can grow ever more formidable with practice, especially when others affirm our rationale. They tell us "It's OK to stick with that job for security," or "Don't be so hard on yourself, we all compromise," or "In a few years it will be time to leave that job or marriage." Many times, neglect harms us more than active sabotage. We put off the gym membership, the diet plan, the religious service, the recovery meeting for another day, the day that never comes—tomorrow. Always tomorrow. The stress of the work routine, family obligations, and unforeseen problems stack up and trap us from acting on solutions. Life is adept at throwing unwanted interruptions at us that distract us from our real goals. We dissipate our energy from a thousand small cuts that leave us unwilling or unable to follow through on our deepest passion or to find the best romantic partner for us. We can be gifted at rationalizing why we are stuck or minimizing our awareness that our spirit is obstructed.

When a police officer knocked on my car window on July 11, 2013 (not the day at the beach), awakening me from a five-hour loss of consciousness, I thought my life was over. I had no memory of parking myself in the middle of a quiet one-way street that in no way looked like a parking space. I was arrested for possession of heroin and released the next morning. The law enforcement officers were kind and took pity on me. They could tell I was not a dealer or a criminal but a very sick man. That almost felt worse. When you can tell someone is thinking: "How can you have done this to yourself?" it awakens that last shred of embarrassment you thought was gone.

The following days brought last-ditch attempts to evade responsibility, followed by resignation and checking into detox. To be clear: the law enforcement charges convinced me to check into treatment—not a desire for help.

In treatment on a psych unit, I detoxed from heavy doses of Xanax, Oxycodone, heroin, and alcohol. It felt like having my skin ripped off, this slow, deep ache in my bones and my mind screaming for the substances it depended on for normalcy. My consciousness reeled at what I had done to it. A hurricane raged within my nervous system as the massive doses of sedatives wore off.

I spent twenty minutes on the phone with my mother trying to record a phone number of a man in AA who I knew was recovering from opiate addiction. My hands trembled and my brain misfired as I scribbled down the number one . . . three . . . seven times as it became clear each set of numbers was equally ineligible. I heard the shaking and tears from my mother as she confronted where I was psychologically. Finally retreating to my room, I sat with a page of hysterical, disjointed nonsense and realized what ownership feels like. I had given the drugs everything, every shred of power. Even my most basic biological functioning depended on their presence. Without them for a single day I found myself helpless.

As many in recovery say, hitting bottom is a gift—if you live through it. There are many kinds of bottoms. Sometimes we come to rock bottom in a marriage, a relationship, or with an out-of-control or abusive child, parent, or sibling. Sometimes a bottom is a job you cannot endure anymore, one that forces you to give up parts of yourself you can't get back. It can be recognizing that your thinking and beliefs have created a life you can no longer tolerate. Or a disdain for the mediocrity of your life.

People have spirited debates about the definition of a bottom. How do you know you've had one or are currently having one? One dictionary definition states that a bottom is "the lowest point or part of something." Another says, "the remotest or inmost point." Perhaps this indicates that a personal bottom is when external and internal consequences penetrate the deepest level of a person, the inmost point: the heart and the spirit.

One definition I like is that a rock bottom is when the pain of staying the same is finally greater than the pain of changing—when you are finally ready to act. It can also be the realization that you are not willing to let that person, drug, job, boss, or home environment stand in your way a minute longer. Even your worst fears and reservations are less painful than continuing to live this way. Reaching a bottom is most closely associated with addictions, but it is an important concept for all people because we all hit bottoms. Addicts have not cornered the market on suffering.

But bottoms also represent the ability to transcend one part of life and begin another. What would we be without that capacity? It is like skipping rocks along the water. We never know why one rock skips endlessly along a lake while another sinks after a single hop. We can continually examine why one person reaches his or her bottom immediately and others don't reach them for years—or never at all. But we all know the feeling of sinking into darkness and praying for an end to one thing and the birth of another.

No matter what shade of darkness you are currently sinking in, know that transcending that darkness is possible. While I was suffering intense body and mind tremors on that psychiatric unit in late July 2013, my emerging truth was to attempt change or die. Sometimes, life, God, or the universe gives us a gift that pulls the show we have created down on our heads. It shows us the futility of our feverish attempts at control and a certainty that this is the end.

The most important thing I have learned is that a bottom can always be a beginning. In some cases, such a massive rearrangement or catastrophe is the ONLY way for there to be a beginning. It is easy to see how an addict or alcoholic has lost the ability to change and often needs a shock.

We can stop listening to the voice that reminds us of our endless options and possibilities every day. The saying is: "We form our habits and then our habits form us." The power of the wrong habits can be devastating, and one of the worst habits is of limitation—limitation in our belief in ourselves and our imagination of obtaining a richer life experience now. Accepting less than we deserve and compromising on the fullness of our life.

Yet I think most people experience forms of learned helplessness that may be more subtle but are just as binding.

If you believe you cannot leave a spouse, family, job, or situation that is destructive to your being, you have a problem. If you have accepted that your internal emotional state is dependent on people or events outside of you, you will always be dependent and disturbed. People delay taking action for years by convincing themselves that now is not the time or by repressing their healthy instincts. Feelings can be dealt with now or later, but believe me, they will be heard. The longer we ignore our feelings, the angrier and more destructive we become.

So, I want to ask: What is the nature of your rock bottom, of this aspect of life that seems intolerable but may be conquered? Is it a person or persons? A job or career that feels meaningless? A part of yourself that won't let you start acting to create something new?

Determining the obstacle and being honest about its nature is critical. You cannot scale a wall without clearly defining what and where it is, and what parts of it you built with your own hands. As a popular motivational speaker says, "Clarity is Power." Figuring out how your efforts or choices contributed to the obstacle is vital as you explore the destruction of the chains binding you to it. I was graced with the gift of desperation in a way that many people are not. Regardless, if you want something different than what you have, you must feed the belief that things can be different. You must listen to that almost imperceptible voice that whispers, "You can be happy at work, you can be valued and loved by your spouse, you can start over. There is more to this life, and you deserve it."

Ignoring or discounting that voice can be accomplished for only so long before it gets too quiet to hear and the years tick by. Don't make it a race from crib to coffin without hearing and living by that voice.

Maybe you are at the end of the first act of your life. You could be ready to abandon a career that ended in failure or gave you success but no joy or meaning. You could learn that as an empty nester, without your kids at home, your life feels meaningless. You could be part of the epidemic of young males who struggled at college or never made it to college. Many people feel lost and hopeless although their life is just starting. Many young adults tell me they see less hope in the world in part due to climate change.

A career, a degree, or a passion put off out of necessity for years—if not decades—could finally be at the edge of your consciousness, ready to break through. We must ask: "What stands between the end of this phase of my life and the beginning of the next?"

It is not a straight line or a single moment. I did not go from sick to cured after July 11, 2013, simply because I never drank alcohol again. I did not walk out of detox floating on joy and grace. A single action to leave a partner, quit a job, or enroll in school may be a critical starting point for a change, but a new phase of life involves a pattern of decisions and attitudes that become pervasive and consistent. "It's always a wonderful thing when you realize you still have the ability to surprise yourself."[1]

---

[1] From the movie *American Beauty*

Many people engaged in spiritual struggle feel an inability to surprise themselves with new behavior. We became stuck beneath the weight of self and are unable to generate new ideas and fresh actions. A new phase is a decision to jump into something new and leave your comfort zone, a process that awakens attributes, skills, and spirit that we had forgotten or never knew we had. Most of us won't make this leap until we are motivated through pain or discomfort.

Yet I strongly believe that if a person determines this moment has come and decides to begin the process of creating a second act in life, it is within their grasp. Our second act lives on the other side of our fear. We don't have to be in excruciating pain to act. When we arrive at the conclusion that this stage of our life must be over . . . needs to be over . . . we must prepare for action with a conviction that is as hard and unbending as steel.

"It's never the changes we want that change everything."
—Junot Diaz

QUESTIONS/EXERCISES

Describe the person, place, job, relationship, or part of you that is negatively affecting your life. How is it obstructing you?

_____
_____
_____
_____
_____
_____
_____
_____
_____
_____
_____
_____
_____
_____
_____
_____
_____

GETTING UP

Leaving detox on July 20, 2013, the air tasted different. I should also say that I tasted the air. That felt new because opioids deprived me of the sensation of having nerves. I remember feeling the breeze on my skin pulsate through my nervous system, the taste of an iced coffee from Dunkin', and the joy of hearing a happy song on the radio. It felt like ten years of feeling came pouring out of and into me. I will never forget the joy of that moment. I felt like a marionette that suddenly found its strings cut: the feeling of freedom was liberating but overwhelming. Learning to move freely physically and spiritually must be relearned.

Additionally, I had a severely disrupted brain reward center that would cause insomnia, generalized anxiety, and wild fluctuations in mood. This lasted six months before some relief arrived. I had to figure out if my life could have a second act because I was still certain of doom. My picture and the articles about my arrest had been published by between eight and fifteen sources. It even appeared on the screen as I watched TV with my fellow patients in detox. I did not have to explain to any of them why I was among them.

My parents took pity on me and allowed me to stay in their home. I coordinated my departure/termination with my school and felt waves of shame over the nature of my leaving, the damage to the reputation of the school, and the example I'd set for the students. I had given blood and sweat to earn the respect of the community and had tarnished that dramatically.

The embarrassment I caused my wife among her family and our neighbors was no less real. My behavior had shaken and harmed people I loved and respected. Sadly, none of that feels real to those of us struggling with addiction. We sell ourselves the fiction that we hurt only ourselves. The reality of escaping into yourself with drugs is that you eventually implode and drastically damage loved ones.

Part of me didn't think I was worth saving. Part of me remained convinced that my addiction to opioids could not be beaten and would kill me. Everything had been ripped away. A world I was on top of—by all external appearances—was flipped on its head. Several towering obstacles stood before me, and each seemed equally unconquerable. My family was gone, my career had imploded, my reputation was tarnished, and my multiple hungry addictions were still lining up to devour me.

Where do I start? People in recovery meetings suggested that "We will believe in you until you believe in yourself."

Getting Up 31

At times we need others to lend us the hope that we can start over. Feeling that we are still alone is untenable if we are to break down the walls we've built. Many suggest starting with faith, praying to whatever you believe in, and more importantly, becoming open to new beliefs and paying attention to your spirit.

It is no surprise that desperate people often find their faith. Years of religious antipathy or the strongest intellectual arguments tumble away in the face of our personal rock bottoms. When depraved unmanageability collides with cold, unforgiving reality . . . when our security is yanked away, we inevitably grasp for something to give it back. In hospital rooms, in wars, in rehabs, a god of any kind suddenly becomes more reasonable and believable. We hope that God is real. But where does our faith go when our crisis is averted? How long does a foxhole prayer remain sincere when the request is resolved? How long will we truly honor the vow we made if God answers us?

My own panicked searching on the web while in the darkness somehow led me to the prayer of St. Michael the Archangel. I printed, read, and carried the prayer with me and sought his protection. I sat at 3 a.m. many nights reading stories of recovery or sitting in darkness outside a church praying to St. Michael to help me last until the next recovery meeting.

I immersed myself in daily recovery meetings, in intensive outpatient treatment, in mandated drug classes, and in community service. My wife and young boys understandably kept a safe distance from me and waited to see what would happen. It is a great trauma to a family when a parent must be removed and is estranged for even a short time. When we regain our sobriety we expect people to be thrilled that we have finally achieved what they begged us to do. We come looking for a celebration and overlook or minimize the mental and emotional damage we have wrought on our loved ones. It is torture to love a person whose best characteristics are swallowed up in a chemical and replaced with selfishness, dishonesty, and unpredictability. People hang on for decades to the ever-fainter memory of the good person they know is still inside a hurricane of dysfunction.

My father has twenty-six years in sobriety attending daily meetings. As a child, I watched his alcoholic behavior and vowed I would never be like that. It created distance that lasted twenty years and wasted precious time. Only when alcohol and heroin brought me to my knees did I understand that I'd become him.

I was just as lost, just as sick, and just as worth saving. Since that time, my empathy for my parents and parents in general has expanded dramatically. Parents usually do the best they can with the resources they have and in response to their own trauma.

Addiction reunited me with my father. Hopefully, the cycle will not extend to my children. My father got sober when I was twelve because he was about to lose his family. He went to treatment and restarted his life, but the trauma of his drinking kept me distant from him for twenty years. Rarely do men get to heal with their fathers in recovery. I have been blessed with eight years attending meetings with my father and hearing regrets and admissions from his soul that I would never have learned without the gift of 12-step recovery. Without those meetings I don't believe my father would be alive. If he were alive, he would not be in my life. Only a community that powerful could tame his disease, heal his wounds, and make him once again a teacher to his children.

If you think of a person's life as a house, sometimes the only hope is to raze the entire structure. Trying to add an extension on a house riddled with black mold is unwise. We are good at adding new parts of our lives on top of an unhealthy, unstable structure. It is understandable, but a shame to do this on top of a structure too fractured to support a new life. Start from the bottom. Go all the way to the root. Don't stop digging until you hit bedrock. Find your foundation stone in a belief in something or someone. Build in support structures—the scaffolding of recovery meetings, therapy, physical exercise routines, meditation, and new and positive friends—to secure your efforts. Find people who are building the kind of life you are seeking. When people try to build a new life with the same group of people in distress, they stagnate and are pulled back down. We must seek new soil and new neighbors.

A man became a good friend to me by offering me work clearing brush and being a ground man in a tree pruning operation. When you suffer a reputational disaster, you learn quickly who your friends really are. By helping me fill hours of frenetic drug craving with work, my friend gave me a fighting chance at surviving my addiction and the demons in my mind. He did this despite my pathetic physical state (zero strength, zero stamina) and the risk of my wasting his time. He gave me something I did not deserve and could not fulfill, but still invested his time and his money into the slimmest of chances. Why would someone do that?

It is a question that can be answered only by someone who has received undeserved grace in their own rock bottom: a hand extended down into the darkness with the faith and knowledge that with enough effort, acceptance, and action, you will be the one reaching down to help the next person. When you have fully renounced your issues, when you are metaphorically lying flat on your back at the bottom of an abyss, that hand from above is the brightest of lights in the dark room of your soul.

When someone's behavior shows us that we are still valuable despite our conclusion of worthlessness, it transmits power into a person who has forgotten both their value and how to regain any power.

I invite you to seek the links between you and other suffering people who are jumping into their next life. I was lifted above my own faltering willpower and damaged brain by a group of spirited people who had been sick and were getting well. When people are at the bottom, for heaven's sake, give them something useful to do. If you are at the bottom, look for something to replace your idleness and avert self-destruction.

After dragging tree branches for a few dollars an hour, and answering phones at a physical therapy office, I finally convinced a rehab to give me a chance as a counselor. I told the director about myself, and he was impressed by my resume. It didn't occur to me to bring up my arrest for heroin nine months earlier or the plethora of news headlines. I assumed in the age of Google that he would know. They would check, right? My resume said Dean of Students at Regis High School, 2008–2013.

A week later I received a call from the rehab's HR director. "Do you know what comes up when I put in your name?" Me: "Yes, I was there. Your director committed to hiring me, and I will not let you down. Please give me a chance to show you." They pushed back for some time but somehow, someone convinced them to give me that first shot back in counseling.

I was nine months sober. Most facilities require a minimum of one year in sobriety before a new hire. With a news trail like mine, I expected it to be a tall order to convince anyone to hire me.

Sometimes we must beg an employer to give us a chance. Make an appeal to them that you will give them something more powerful than whatever negative press or record you are escaping. If you are sincere and persistent, you will eventually find a person who respects the power and grace of redemption. Maybe it will take three tries, maybe nine. Do not accept failure.

I was making $112,000 in my last year in school administration. Now I was making $17 an hour, and it was the happiest year I can remember.

I felt more fully alive than I had in years. I realized more deeply than I ever had how little money correlates with my living in purpose. When you take nothing for granted, you are filled with a joy for the sounds, smells, and experiences in life. To be able to show up and help people again after such a profound fall from grace was liberating. It brought me back to the service I felt in my high school, the psychiatric hospital, the school, and now the rehab with court-ordered substance use clients.

What was paramount to making that new beginning? Belief in something is paramount. And when belief is tentative or overcome by doubt, as mine often was, we can write our new story only one day—or one moment—at a time. Even getting a few days of productive work under your belt is critical to see yourself do it. Many of us feel we must see evidence that a new approach will work before beginning, but with a second act of life, often, we must begin in order to see it. Only action creates a new path. You can plan and think about change for years, but that first concrete action is what makes it real. If you want something different, take the first step and hold onto your conviction that things *must* be different for you.

Most of us lose momentum when our first attempts don't reap immediate fruit. If you decide that the path is not a choice but a necessity, and you dedicate all your resolve to following it through, a new life will find you.

On the next page, write down what you dream the next part of your life can be. If you believe it, don't allow anyone to block your pursuit. List the necessary actions to make your dream real and make yourself accountable.

Then, share your goals with someone you respect who will hold you to your commitments. Dare to believe things can be created anew in your life.

QUESTIONS/EXERCISES

A Second Act for My Life
What do I want Part Two of my life to look and feel like?
How do I want it to be different?

_____
_____
_____
_____
_____
_____
_____
_____
_____
_____
_____
_____
_____
_____
_____
_____
_____

What actions are the starting point for making this real?

GETTING UP, CONTINUED

The phoenix attracts me as a symbol because its resurrection implies pain. As melodramatic as that may sound, it has always been my experience that recreation involves suffering. We do not create massive change without struggle. I like the image of the phoenix, especially because you cannot necessarily tell where the fire or destruction ends and the creation and resurrecting spirit begins.

We often think of people as being in darkness or in light. That polarization runs into trouble in real life. Some parts of our growth and rebirth are directly tied to the darkness we are fighting to overcome. You cannot have the glory of a recreated phoenix without your demons fueling the fire. You can fly high in recovery only after you have sunk to tremendous lows. If you desire rebirth or recreation, you must understand how the damage you have caused yourself can be used for creation.

Carl Jung (1875–1961) is perhaps the most famous psychiatrist in history and made unique contributions to recovery from psychiatric and spiritual disease.

> "Unfortunately there can be no doubt that man is, on the whole, less good than he imagines himself or wants to be. Everyone carries a shadow, and the less it is embodied in the individual's conscious life, the blacker and denser it is. If an inferiority is conscious, one always has a chance to correct it. Furthermore, it is constantly in contact with

other interests, so that it is continually subjected to modifications. But if it is repressed and isolated from consciousness, it never gets corrected."

—Carl Jung

I repressed my shadows for years and consuming vodka would release it onto anyone unlucky enough to be in my vicinity. Repressing the shadow within only creates vastly more powerful shadows, guiding us blindly from below the surface. If we are to conquer the internal civil war we must face and integrate the dark that lives within us. Also accept that transforming this darkness into becoming a whole person takes time, sincerity, and the ability to tolerate some pain.

I realized that I had restarted my life and was on safer ground when my belief in myself grew; when it was no longer fragile and fleeting. Running therapy groups at the inner-city Bridgeport, Connecticut, residential rehab in 2015 was an important beginning. I had seen my arrest and rock bottom as a big deal in the wealthier area where I attended meetings. What I learned as a counselor in the inner city is that my story was a Disney World version of drug and alcohol dependence. What I had lived for five years was, for many people, their entire lives.

The levels of abuse, trauma, and broken homes running like barbed wire through those inner-city people's lives was catastrophic. It was completely understandable why so many people used drugs to medicate. There was no way to minimize their pain and the depth of the fractures in their lives, spiritually, mentally, and physically.

It is less clear why those of us with less economic hardship or trauma get pulled into the darkness as well. People are tempted to say, "What have *you* got to complain about?"

In the late '70s, Canadian psychologist Dr. Bruce Alexander conducted what were known as the Rat Park experiments in laboratories at Simon Fraser University in British Columbia. The research showed that rats dependent on opiates can withdraw from drugs and become abstinent should a social and open environment be provided to them. Dr. Alexander broke new ground in arguing that for humans, unlike rats, the reality of our environment is less important than our perception of it.

If we perceive our world as scary or confining, we will often pursue relief and be at high risk for addictive chemicals and mental health issues. In Connecticut, I saw many people whose lives were literally like the cages in the Rat Park experiments: unstable housing, poverty, abuse, arrest records—zero resources. Despite that, some of them showed they could transcend the limitations of their lives.

All I had to do was transform my perception to see that my environment could be wide open to possibility. In truth, it had mostly been wide open. To help these men transform their perception while continuing to face tremendous economic, legal, housing, and mental health issues was more of a challenge.

I met a man from a ghetto in Hartford, Connecticut. I'll call him Michael. When Michael's wife ran off with his child he lost what little control he had in his life and fell into heroin addiction and active schizophrenia. After bouncing around homeless and in shelters for years, he was given a state bed at our facility. He was the nicest man I'd ever met. He carried himself with gentleness and grace. Despite a constant hum of voices no one else could hear, he displayed kindness and poured his creativity into art. Sketching away at intricate portraits and designs expressed his struggle, but more importantly, his hope. The artistic results of his unbeatable optimism continue to hang on my office wall. One proudly displays, in a thousand vibrant colors, "BE PROUD OF WHO YOU ARE."

His issues could not stop him from perceiving good in the world and expressing kindness to everyone he met. He helped teach me that my addiction was just a small taste of what millions experience for decades.

It also shows that the extent of our suffering is immaterial. Whether it's substances, relationships, anxiety, or depression, we isolate ourselves when we believe that we're alone in our suffering or unique in the extent of it. The disease of comparison blocks our peace. Deciding that someone else's story is better or worse than ours, that our addiction or problem is different from theirs, keeps us alone on our island.

Another man—I'll call him Ray—was released after twenty years incarcerated. He'd spent ages twenty to forty in jail. A substantial part of his life was taken away because he got drunk one night and hit a man in a fight. The man's head hit the curb and he passed away. It was the first time Ray drank. It's hard to explain why the balance of justice acts as it does because I drove intoxicated and made dangerous decisions thousands of times and got away with far less serious consequences. Some of us get many chances at a second act in life while others get one chance or no mercy.

The emerging strength I found in my recovery was reinforced daily by my own program and the grace I witnessed in the men at that residential facility.

The same way a single young sprout can grow out of a dirty garbage heap, among damaged people, a little support yields abundant moments of grace and dignity. It was wonderful to see that beauty blossom in an environment that should have been too ugly to produce it. I saw see peoples' spirits return, and mine with it. There is nothing more uplifting than seeing light return to a person's once empty eyes.

You cannot doubt the spiritual once you have witnessed emptiness ignite into light and belief. Cold, withdrawn, and angry becomes open, creative, spirited. Is the light still present in your eyes? If the light has dimmed or died out in you, think about what is smothering that light. A myriad of things drown out our spirits: a relationship that prevents us from being our authentic selves, a job or career that strangles the spirit, even our refusal to listen to our spirit.

My counseling journey took me from the residential facility to intensive outpatient treatment and then to counseling at a Christian recovery program before starting my own private practice. The Christian organization had a profound effect on me. I was counseling many men who were homeless or had few to no resources. Crack cocaine, heroin, crystal meth, and PCP are the stuff of nightmares.

What they do to men and women is worse than any hell that can be imagined.

These men were at rock bottom and many knew it. I saw the defeat in their eyes. The trauma that had swirled together—a mixture of poverty, community, mental health, and family influence—had produced a perfect recipe for drugs to become the only power in their life. Men come in with rotten teeth and emaciated spirits. By the time they left, many had new sets of teeth they proudly showed off. They had gained a dozen—or dozens—of pounds. Their brains and nervous systems had regulated to some extent. They were calmer in thought and speech. I saw an improved ability to reflect on and have wiser perspectives on their pasts and larger visions for their futures.

Many times, by discharge, those emaciated spirits had been refilled. The real challenge was in teaching people how to continuously refill the reservoir so they can be lifted out of their quest for happiness or pleasure through drugs or material things.

Many rehab patients had gained weight, health, and confidence. They felt cured—that the reservoir was full and they were back in control. This is a dangerous miscalculation, as the millions of people who have cycled through rehabs across the country can attest. *Nobody* is cured after rehab.

We must help people to see the truth of what actually helps. Two methods are asking for help and surrendering to something, be it a god, treatment center, group of people, or set of beliefs while being surrounded by others who are sincere about recovering. Fellowship is critical in balancing the limits of self-knowledge and willpower, as are discussions of and invitations to spirituality.

Spirituality is urgently sought in a community of people brought to their knees by a chemical they're addicted to. They suffer tremendous despair and soul sickness and seek something that can give them back their power. They gave the drugs power—and look what happened.

You may have given your spouse, partner, or job your power. If we once again conclude that self-knowledge or external factors give us power, our reservoir will drain again, slowly or rapidly, and it will be empty soon. Understanding the refueling process properly is paramount to continuing to recover from any profound personal struggle.

Throughout this stage of recovery, I had a loving wife who had my back. Despite the lies and damage wrought by addiction, she continued to support and love me. The level of some people's loyalty can never be explained, but it was a miracle I did not deserve. In my addiction I had been emotionally unavailable to my children and missed valuable time. Now I could give my presence to those two young boys whose laughter and smiles filled my spirit again.

Feeling like a stable man and father again, I sought to ensure that I'd never lose that feeling again. I took on service commitments, including returning to the detox center I'd attended in 2013. Returning there every week to hear the rock bottom stories of good people and be reminded of my own served a powerful purpose. Remembering where you come from and who you are is critical to not backsliding.

Every time I get up to leave an inpatient psychiatric unit and the magnetic locks on the door open, I am flooded with the euphoria of freedom. Freedom through recovery from drugs and alcohol. Freedom from the tyrannical rule of the ego and negative thinking. Freedom from limits. Transitioning from a death's-door heroin addict to a counselor with a private practice and a loving family made me realize I can't *ever* forget that anything is possible.

I want to ask you what you still think your limits are. Write down what things, people, or parts of you limit or constrain you from increased freedom. To surpass them you must know them.

❖ ❖ ❖

QUESTIONS/EXERCISES

What are your limits?
(Things, people, your own thinking)

In 2015 I decided to open a private practice. I hung up my shingle and got credentialed with multiple insurance companies. I know what it is like to pay out of pocket for therapy; often, I could not afford it either. Remaining in network with insurers is an important value to me; many people need access to good mental health care that is financially out of reach. People need quality helpers. There is nothing special about me, but I can serve and so can you. I can give everything I have to adolescents, adults, and couples who are suffering.

When I sit in the breach with someone who is facing and being enveloped in their personal disaster, I can be with them in love and fellowship. When people are not alone in their suffering, even for an hour, it has a powerful effect in joining with and lifting them. Most people want help. They want someone to understand. How far we can all come with the art of listening!

> *"We think we listen, but very rarely do we listen with real understanding, true empathy. Yet listening, of this very special kind, is one of the most potent forces for change that I know."*
> —Carl Rogers

Learning to listen can be game-changing in all our relationships. People in counseling come alive when they see we truly care and are with them in the moment. Many people feel no one is hearing them. In the distracted world we live in, how often can we claim to be focused enough to truly hear our loved ones? We must get past peoples' words, listen to their emotions, and deeper than that, their spirits. Learning to listen in my own life has proven indispensable to creating stronger bonds.

Reflecting on the contrast between the addict in the newspaper headlines in 2013 and the person I am now feels like being in a dream. I simultaneously feel embarrassment, acceptance, and inspiration. I am father to a thirteen-year-old and eleven-year-old boy and a two-year-old girl. I have joined with my father in a life of recovery and in hope that my children never again see the monster Mr. Hyde triggered by alcohol or opium.

I make a living manifesting that role, which was always my greatest dream: being a clinician in private practice. I have the honor of earning a living by sitting in sacred quiet with people and being a helper and healer. What about my story suggests I deserve that?

I knew good men and woman now dead by opiates or alcohol who wanted their sobriety as badly as I did and were putting in the work to save their lives. With addiction you can win the fight every day for a decade only to have one bad misstep send you to your death. Some of us are permitted more slips than others. God only knows why.

I could not now be more grateful for the life I have been given out of the ashes of a living death. I have peace in my head and an active link flowing between my head and my heart. While addicted, all I heard were the contents of my head—90 percent fear and anxiety on a permanent loop. In living differently and finding faith I have found positive emotions again and self-love. I can now walk through the days responding and acting from both head and heart, using both reason and warmth to respond to the world.

I also gave up on perfectionism, and I strongly suggest you do the same. Demanding perfection is the fastest way to never enjoy or accept yourself. Demand progress but celebrate your efforts and the gains made. A big part of any recovery is renegotiating the relationship with your self.

The following sections contain tools and resources for starting over, getting better, and rediscovering your spirit.

✦ ✦ ✦

FEAR

If you let it, fear will take everything from you. It will undercut every good thing in you, every certainty and conviction you hold dear. If you attempt a restart in your life, you have no choice but to face fear head on and to initiate action.

I write this for people who know the pain of overt self-consciousness: bloody, dismaying conscious observations and judgments of self. I can't tell you accurately how much time I've wasted in my life worrying about things that never came to pass. For me, a stench of terror formed the subtle background of all things. I constantly projected that something would go wrong.

My brain was gifted at creating several versions of how badly any situation would play out: The presentation would go sideways, the date would be horrible, the person I liked wouldn't like me, and I should be concerned because my brain *is* seeing the future.

Of course, *it only seemed* that my projections could or would become real events. With years of reflection on self and discussions with others, I have seen evidence that the brain's "crystal ball" is deeply flawed. It has cracks running through every part that distort most of the images it reflects. The majority of our projections are as illusory as they are plentiful. To give power to that fearful and hysterical part of our brain is to doom many of our days to anxious preoccupation and ruined moments.

When we accept our fearful predictions of failure, several dangerous things occur. From that moment on we proceed with doubt and lack of attention to the people and opportunities we are interacting with *now*. We allocate mental energy and crucial focus to ruminating over a past situation. Even if it's 15 percent of our focus, that is more than enough to disrupt everything else we are doing in the moment. Taking that amount from your marriage, your relationship with your kids, your best friend, or job is causing some amount of neglect to all of them. If that 15 percent is used every day to anticipate terrible events in future days, it's no wonder your days are not going great. The more you accept the predictions and allow the brain free reign to rehearse them endlessly, the more the brain magnifies the volume and number of future calamities.

Our projections are only trying to protect us, to safeguard our physical safety and our ego. Our attempts to safeguard the ego most illustrate how delusional this "warning system" can become. We may predict an insult coming, or a confrontation with a friend or coworker, client, disgruntled service provider, contractor, neighbor, or boss. Who knows what makes us predict this in the first place? Sometimes the tone of a voicemail, text, or email message alerts us that a conflict may be coming. Or a presentation is scheduled, and we identify several people or situations that could sabotage or humiliate us on the big day. The smallest, most questionable perceptions can set off a conclusion of trouble approaching.

Then again, there are times we *should* worry. Sometimes real confrontations and necessary disputes will happen. The real question is: how can we downshift our mental engine so our future becomes subservient to our present self? We may never fully succeed in eradicating future anxiety and the instinct of the mind to predict negativity.

We need to reestablish dominance of self through grounding techniques. To be grounded means to feel more secure in self and less controlled or lost in mental chatter or preoccupation. To drop physical and mental weight into the body and heart, not just let a neurotic brain drag us around. To find a reasonable balance.

Meditation and mindfulness practices are the best friends of the worried mind. I used Xanax for twenty years to try to eradicate worry. If you are doing the same, realize that the longer you depend on a medication to suppress worry, the more challenging it will be to inevitably face your worry. Because you eventually will face it. When you do, you'll start to learn emotional and mental regulation at the emotional age you were when you began taking the drug. For me, that was twenty years old. Being emotionally armed at forty with the skill level of a twenty-year-old was daunting.

Pushing down fear and anxiety causes it to powerfully grow and mutate. Here is the trick: Sometimes the self cannot ground the self. I say that as a person who has wrestled with the anxiety of what *might* be coming for forty years and often found my efforts unsuccessful.

We can and need to build our identification with our *Self* as distinct from the mind. If not, we are always sleeping in bed with an assassin. Practicing meditation is a vital way to connect with and build the link with your deeper self as the mind becomes calmer and quieter. Self-affirmations are also useful in building self-esteem and the muscles needed to tune the mind out.

The mind is like a child with ADHD you've loaded with sugar and then invited to expound on everything it knows. The more you show interest and encourage it, the louder it will get. You must show the mind what input is not useful and that you are less and less interested in its prophecies. Within three months, a fear that ruined an entire night could be a thirty second interchange with the mind.

Mind: "You have that appointment at 9 a.m. tomorrow. That person has acted cold toward you in the past; she seems to have an attitude. Perhaps she thinks you are not good at what you do. Maybe you are a fraud."

Self: "Thanks for the input. Not interested. Fuck off."

The original incident that ruined a whole night would likely fill pages narrating the battle between self and mind. I'm sure you have had some internal monologues that have dragged on for days. I am not suggesting change will happen so easily. As you become clearer in giving your self power and moderating the brain's input, you will stop generating as much fear.

If your brain generates less fear and spends less time in the amygdala, the brain center that generates fear, you will weaken the neural networks related to danger and all the ways things go wrong. You will access fewer negative issues from the past that constantly feed your projections.

The less you drive down those roads, the more they fade. The more quickly you ignore and dismiss the negative prognostications of the mind, the more you remain in the self and the moment. Imagine how much better you could live if you can do that! Take back that daily 15 percent of worry and put it to good effect in noticing what is actually happening in the world.

Begin to focus less on negativity and more on positive outcomes. Where you may have had three negative versions of a future event, now you can imagine at least one positive outcome. The Self can help train the brain in *what* to look for. If you search deeply inside yourself for what you seek and are expecting, your mind will take that direction and search for it.

Decide today to commit to rise above fear. Just for today. To decide is to cut off the options for worry. Coupled with that decision, direct your mind toward several positive goals/predictions. Review a few events happening today and instruct yourself to predict good possibilities. They are as likely to happen as most of the horror shows your brain writes. Accept how unknowable any predictions of the future are and how worthless it is to expend your energy on them.

Look for positive outcomes and engage in positive action rather than focusing on negative projections. A few days of vigorous, focused work can far exceed the losses of months of projecting and imagining. If you can admit that ingesting drugs or alcohol over the last few years is precisely what has led you to an obstacle or rock bottom, then accept that radically different actions and attitudes will lead you somewhere far better.

Understand how to create good results in the future by choosing excellence / mindfulness now. Create fullness in this day only. Tap into your spirit through your relationships and passions—through feeling meaning in your life and seeing how you deserve to feel your worth. To lose the fear of tomorrow, fall in love with today. Make it your mission to place all your energy on what you are doing in this moment.

"He did each single thing as if he did nothing else."
—Charles Dickens

Practice entering a state of flow (feeling fully immersed in an action) to continuously join in harmony during any activity or circumstance. Find activities that allow a sense of flow. Chopping wood, cleaning, walking, swimming, writing—anything that gives you relief from mental chatter and shows you an alternative state of being. If you can practice and strengthen that grounded sense of *being*, you can conquer a wayward mind.

Then you must practice. Do repetitions everyday of practices that boost the self and tame the mind. Design specific practices: daily readings or inspirations, meditations at the same times every day, a recovery meeting every day, positive self-affirmations. Play with, practice, and explore to find the practices that work best. Say to yourself in the car or in front of the mirror: "I give power to self, not mind, I give power to self, not mind; my focus is just today, I am here now." Do whatever keeps moving you in the right direction. Hold yourself responsible for that movement because no one else can.

This will help you forge a healthier relationship with your mind, bringing it into closer obedience to the wishes of your deeper self and spirit. You cannot do that if you continue to allow your mind to endlessly ruminate on the future rather than harnessing it to focus on today. Use it in its proper place, as a servant to make today better for your self. Even if it's only 5 percent better today, that 5 percent improvement to your interactions with your spouse, your friends, or an important work call will infuse more energy and quality into all of them.

Chronic worry inhibits our daily personal interactions. The brain cannot help but produce "seeds"—some dark, some light. To pretend that you can't control what it produces is to allow it to continue to infect your present and create a degraded future. Find your power in planting a positive environment within yourself. It is the best way to weaken your fear. Take care of your *self* by harnessing the mind to support and empower you.

❖ ❖ ❖

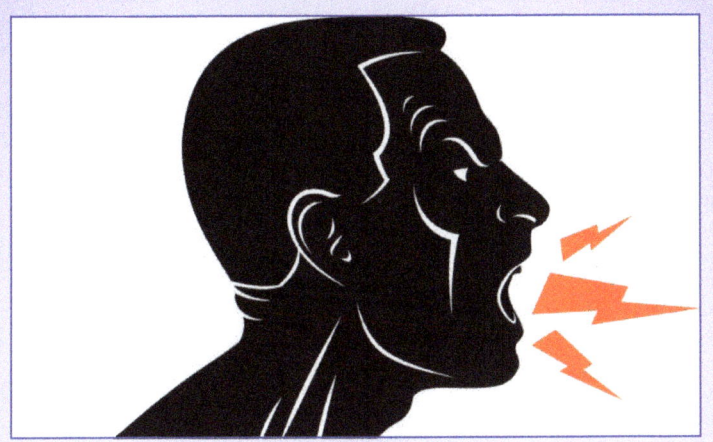

THE VOICE

"Many people spend their whole lives doing their best to follow the coaching, guidance, and warnings of the inner critic. Society supports this. However, if you choose to pursue inner work—the search for understanding who you are, what your life means, and what reality is—you are by necessity setting yourself directly in conflict with your judge. To explore what you believe, what you experience, why you act and feel the way you do, is to question the authority of the judge. To bring the underpinnings of your psychological reality (how you think and feel) into consciousness means potentially replacing those assumptions and beliefs with direct knowledge. This would mean experiencing that your conscious awareness can begin to take the place of accepted standards and beliefs. Then you don't need to be guided, limited, and controlled by the unconscious through your judge."

—Byron Brown

We cannot move forward on this path of change without addressing *the voice*. You know, the "you are not good enough for that . . . you are not good enough for them . . . you are a fraud" *voice*. The "don't take that risk, don't be vulnerable, who are you to be happy?" *voice*. The "don't expect more of yourself, be terrified by your dreams, and stay safe and comfortable" *voice*. Right now, it may be dormant or very quiet, but we all have it. In psychology, many call it the inner critic or judge. To many of us it is an assassin that shoots down our hopes and a brute that pummels our spirits.

When the spirit stretches out of its protection like a snail coming out of its shell, that *voice* will strike. It shouts warnings, cultivates fears, and sows doubts about everything you want that is good and pure. It seems to want a life in the shell, protected and dull. It can keep you inside your shell or shield your dreams from you for years. I picture our unfulfilled dreams like a sea of neglected, sad seeds with untold riches forever unrealized. We must remember that a two-hundred-foot-tall redwood starts in a seed under an inch long. What if you keep your dreams in the dark your whole life? What if you carry them to your grave, never fully exposing them to the light?

That voice comes from the fear center of our brain, coupled with trauma and doubts from earlier life experiences. Parents or authority figures may have convinced you to doubt yourself. Perhaps peer groups activated insecurities that haunt you to this day. If you have bought into their conclusions, if you continue to grant those conclusions power, you must challenge and depose that voice.

Ask yourself: What would it be like if that voice were positive? What if when during a search for a new job it said, "You can do any of these jobs well," or as you peruse dating profiles, it said, "Someone out there is going to be very lucky to have you."

Ask yourself: What is stopping the voice from saying encouraging things? Write down all the reasons it spouts negative pronouncements. These reasons are lumps of coal that can be transformed into diamonds. The reasons for your doubt, the experiences that give power to your "judge" can be reexamined and remade into action plans. They can become burning motivations to help you prove you can live fully.

Whatever happened to you in the past is not a reason to do less, to not try, to play it safe. Don't let that negative voice coach you. When we transform what the coach says from "Get off the field; you suck" to "Get out there and have fun, because you have so much to put on the field," we can win at literally everything. Taking risks and following our passions is possible only to the extent that we can act, despite that voice's criticisms and warnings.

Look for all the ways you hear it. Keep a notebook with you and spend a day recording every doubt, observation, warning, admonishment, limitation, or reproach. Determine what the voice wants from and for you. Open yourself to outside observation and make yourself accountable by discussing your inner critic with a counselor or trusted friend.

There is something powerful and tangible about verbalizing our fears and negative beliefs to another human being.

Express that "This is what my inner critic is telling me." For example: "This is how my life will be if I continue to give it power over my actions . . . I will stay with him/her . . . I won't leave that damn job . . . I will never ask them for a date . . . I will never try that activity, that dream . . . I will never experience freedom from that voice."

Hold onto that last statement for a moment. What if you never experience freedom from that voice? What if you allow it to keep you hostage, to rule over you like the cruelest of kidnappers? Do you want to remain powerless to overcome that negative voice?

Don't worry about shouting down your inner critic, or heaping scorn and hostility on it. That tends to empower it. Don't meet anger and judgment with more anger and judgment. Instead, seek to empower your positive inner coach. Invite it back to the throne room in your head and give *it* power.

Start now to reinforce that inner coach in small ways. If this proves challenging, start with positive affirmations through any good meditation app and let the coach be surrounded by the positive messages it needs to accept and develop. Immerse yourself in the encouraging, affirming voice that still resides within you. It doesn't matter how buried the affirming voice is or how monstrous you have made your inner critic.

Dig out the coach slowly and with purpose. Try it on for size. Think of what you are most avoiding due to a lack of belief or confidence in yourself. Tell yourself you can have a positive coach. Visualize how far your dreams can manifest with a voice that offers wholehearted encouragement and support.

Most importantly, dare to believe you deserve this encouragement because your critic has deprived you of your rightful inheritance. It is telling you not to unwrap the presents you were given that are your birthright. What the critic *should* really be saying is: "You have every right to develop these gifts, and no right to think so little of yourself." The *voice* should not be working to keep you trapped in a shell. It needs to lead you into the full light of becoming *you*—fully and authentically *you*.

If you take nothing else from this book, promise yourself that your inner critic will never be your overlord again. Resolve to conquer it by hand-feeding your inner coach with encouragement, approval, and love. Even if the critic remains within you, let it be a passive observer or an inconsequential bystander to the glories you will attain. Should you invest enough in your coach, your judge will inevitably lose authority and be heard less. That negative booming *voice* will become a manageable distraction and finally, an inaudible whisper.

One day, you will hear only the voice you were born to hear: the voice that convinces you of your profound worth and finally grants you the ability to act like it. On that day, you will know the freedom that has always been waiting for you, and ask yourself: "Why on earth did I listen to that idiot *voice* for so long?"

❖ ❖ ❖

MENTAL HEALTH

"It's okay to feel unstable. It's okay to disassociate. And, it's okay to hide from the world. And, it's okay to need help. It's okay not to be okay. Your mental illness is not a personal failure."
—Unknown

Our 16th president, Abraham Lincoln, teaches us a great deal about mental health. Scholarship has displayed the depth of the depression that Lincoln struggled with throughout his life. Robert Wilson, who was elected, as was Lincoln, to the Illinois state legislature in 1836, wrote of Lincoln: "Still when by himself, he told me that he was so overcome with mental depression, that he never dare carry a knife in his pocket."

Lincoln once wrote to his law partner: "I am now the most miserable man living. If what I feel were equally distributed to the whole human family, there would not be one cheerful face on the earth. Whether I shall ever be better I can not tell; I awfully forebode I shall not. To remain as I am is impossible; I must die or be better, it appears to me."

This was a man who knew chronic and debilitating darkness.

Scholars seem to agree that by the middle of his life Lincoln had largely resolved his struggle with wanting to kill himself and was inspired to try and live for something. However, he continued to struggle with serious discomfort and staggering depressive spells. Lincoln was treated for depression throughout his life and took medication to help him with his moods and depression. In his forties he found a mission in which to dedicate and arouse all his energy and passion. That mission was the annihilation of slavery in our country. It seemed to have been a big enough a mission to conquer his intense psychic pain and make it worthwhile to hang on. Despite the grandeur of such a figure, Lincoln's successes were not possible without his struggles.

If we can find something worth fighting for, our pain and sickness will be the gateway to our eventual accomplishments. We must find something strong and brilliant enough to act as a searchlight, even in our darkest moments.

We live on a crowded, warming planet with increasing wars and political divisions. Our mental health must be addressed and cared for with conviction. Before the pandemic, 8.5 percent of U.S. adults reported being depressed.

That number of depressed adults has risen to 27.8 percent[2] as the country struggles with Covid-19.

Additionally, the national rate of suicidal ideation has risen every year since 2010/2011. Over half of adults with mental illness receive no treatment, totaling over 27 million adults in the United States.[3] Increasingly, young people feel more hopeless about the state of the world and the climate crisis. The same source finds that over 60 percent of youth with major depression do not receive any mental health treatment. This is the tip of the iceberg in how much suffering occurs when it comes to our mental health.

The pandemic has created what is rightly called a mental health epidemic. The mass disconnection of Covid isolation has pushed many at-risk people off the cliff and many well-functioning people to the edge. It has also made some long-suffering individuals feel strangely better because so many people were experiencing something like the intense suffering they have lived with for years. It has rattled the population by reminding us of our lack of control and fraying many of our social connections.

It is tragic that mental health continues to be a source of stigma. Many might agree that some progress has been made in education about mental health, with brave individuals fighting against stigma. The purpose of discussion for this book is how mental health issues affect a person's bottoms/lows and can paralyze or derail attempts for a

---

2 The State of Mental Health in America | Mental Health America (mhanational.org)
3 *Ibid.*

second act/recovery in life. Our mental health NEEDS to be addressed.

How could it not be helpful to examine, with trained, intelligent professionals, the workings of our thinking, beliefs, and decisions and whether they are working or sabotaging our every step? How can we be overconfident enough to think we possess as much knowledge and insight about ourselves and the world as we need? Why don't we welcome transparency, request others' informed perceptions about our struggles, and accept help in leading us out of the dark?

That our ego convinces us that we must figure our issues out alone is part of the problem, as is the shame in feeling that asking for help indicates weakness. We hide pain and discomfort while putting ourselves through the endless labyrinth of our psyche trying to solve everything in secret.

Many people in their rock bottom of depression, anxiety, addiction, divorce, etc., are overwhelmed with the conviction that "I am alone in my pain." We as a culture need to prove to people that no one need be alone. If we more openly encourage the sharing of pain, struggle, and recovery, we show the universality of struggle and normalize it. There is perhaps no greater feeling of relief than the first time you really feel you are not alone.

I have spent decades searching out the nooks and crannies of "me" island, looking under every rock and the bottom of every cave. There is nothing new there—or at least, nothing else I will find until I enlist other searchers to help in my own rescue.

Mental health

"People can take you to a place inside yourself that you can't go by yourself."
—**Les Brown**

What is blocking you from inviting a psychologist, counselor, social worker, priest, spiritual adviser or other loving human being to survey your inner island and offer some help? If pride prevents you, how much suffering are you willing to take? How many years or decades do we examine the same maps before realizing they can be interpreted only with others? It's as if our issues exist in the dark—and light is shed upon them only when we invite helpers and teachers to assist us in interpreting them. The purpose of this section is to convince you to enlist help and open yourself to someone.

Receiving mental health care can be hard. To admit to and shine light on the problems we are ashamed of and embarrassed to share can be excruciating. It takes hard work to receive counseling and therapy. There are breakthroughs and occasional rapturous moments, but to investigate and rebuild the self we need true perseverance. We need to hang onto the vision we have for Act Two of our life.

Write out the changes you would like to see in your mental health. How do you want your life and functioning to be different after receiving care?

◆ ◆ ◆

QUESTIONS/EXERCISES

Gains I want from mental health care:

Bring this list to a mental health professional. Use a validated website like Psychology Today or call your insurance company to search for providers. Check their credentials, read through their profiles, and make sure they are a good fit for you. After reading through their profile and approach to therapy, ask yourself:

"Does this fit with who I am and what will be helpful to me?"

"Do they show a specialty in one of my main problem areas and a therapy style I am familiar with?"

Finding the right fit is important. If you feel uncomfortable with your provider, despite the inconvenience of finding someone new, it's worth making a different selection. Make a list of your top questions for the provider and be sure to get answers. *It is your life.*

While all professionals attempt to be helpful, some may turn out to be a bad fit. I promise there will be another professional who has the words, skills, and empathy needed to help you restart your life. So bring your statements above to a professional and make the leap. Realize that whatever your issue is, it will take time to work out. Not days or weeks—more often months or years. That's OK, as long as you are progressing toward the right destination.

For me, there is a sacredness to being a therapist: to sit in a room unraveling someone's story and to be given the keys to their internal life. It is a gift and an honor to be let in and invited to influence their narrative. My father, in his role as a literary agent, spent forty years helping people craft and perfect their stories. My job as a therapist is nearly identical: helping people examine the stories they tell about themselves.

What is your narrative of your past and what happened to get you here? Reading through those lines carefully with a therapist is sure to turn up some errors or incorrect "edits" you've made that warped aspects of your story and how you are continuing to write it.

We are living our present days based on a story formed in part on incorrect perceptions and incomplete conclusions from our past. None of us can know the extent of our mistaken conclusions until we gain the courage to shine a searchlight over our past. Correcting our story is paramount to our restarting our life. We need to reframe it as a story of survival and resurrection rather than of guilt and resentments. You have been writing this story of your life, and if you want it to change, pick a good therapist and get to work. You do not have to be Abraham Lincoln, but you do need to pick something worth living for.

◆ ◆ ◆

NEUROPLASTICITY

*"Any man could, if he were so inclined,
be the sculptor of his own brain."*
—Santiago Ramon y Cajal,
Advice for a Young Investigator

For several hundred years, a prevailing theory has been that the brain's ability to change in adulthood is limited; that after young adulthood the brain matter present is all a person has to work with. This has contributed to the belief that the brain does not physically change in adulthood, which contributes to our belief that human behavior is fixed. This meant that as adults, we were unlikely to radically change our behavior and brain structure. Many people concluded that their addiction / mental health was untreatable. "Oh well," they might have said, "this is how

I am. I've tried to change for years and I keep failing. I'll just accept it."

But over the last twenty years, research has shown that we can use our thinking and behavior to change the brain, both physically and functionally. Many people have demonstrated their ability to enact tremendous change throughout their lives, but having science back up and illuminate this message is powerful. It helps empower all of us to fight rigid thinking and behavior and avoid being resigned to limits on our ability to change.

Now, what we choose to believe can materialize, not just in abstract thoughts or intentions, but written in the code of new neural networks and displayed in the areas of growth in our lives.

When we seek a new phase in life, we must embrace neuroplasticity as a powerful tool. But how do we embrace the new when the old crushes us? How do we loosen the grip of habit and unlearn limitation? When we can't let go of any part of old habits we must eliminate them all. This is easier said than done. We must start. We must leave one relationship or send out one resume or take one kickboxing class in our pursuit of improvement.

If we are staying in our comfort zone to avoid pain, we thwart the total commitment needed for success. We must take those first steps while holding fast to the belief that our mindset *can* be changed. We must be willing to accept sacrifices and discomfort—sometimes indefinitely.

The mind resists change. It's like a city on a hill trying to protect itself from attack or chaos. In our defense of the status quo we build up defenses and resist even the most beneficial changes. How often do we delay for months—or even years—taking actions that can free us from a major weight we know is bringing us down?

When we finally let go, we say to a therapist or loved one: "I can't believe it took me that long to leave him" or "Why did I waste eight years slaving away at that job?" How can we accept and suffer an emotional "splinter" in our life that is so visible? Perhaps that's where neuroplasticity can come in.

Many of us were raised with a sense that little change is possible in our lives. Even for those for whom that is less true, by adulthood many have limited their expectations of themselves. Frustrations in relationships, moods, behaviors, and thinking sets a ceiling for us that seems impenetrable.

At some point our belief in our ability to manifest new, flexible behavior hardens like super glue. Flexible and powerful becomes rigid and weak. Whether this is caused quickly by an addiction, a traumatic experience, interpersonal betrayal, or it occurs slowly by a loss of freedom over a long, numbing arc is almost irrelevant. Once it has occurred, we face the same dilemma: How do we "unstick" ourselves and make a leap to more spontaneity and creativity? What if you could let down the wall between what you have and what you could have? What is the thing you will not consider is possible for your life?

Look at the rationalizations that block the first door in a series of hallways leading up and out of mediocrity. Walking through the first door is critical to showing yourself change is possible. Many ask for evidence that a thing can be realized before they are willing to act, but we must imagine the thing powerfully enough to act in order to produce the evidence. This is understandably difficult. Nevertheless, change always starts with seeing that change is possible.

Prove to yourself the power of change. Do something extraordinary. Turn your daily habits upside down. Set your alarm for a different time, go out for breakfast instead of eating at home, talk on a work call when you're normally silent, take a different route to and from work, have dinner at a new place in a new town, call a friend you haven't spoken to in years . . . even brush your teeth with the opposite hand. As silly or trivial as this may sound, it is a remarkably useful place to start.

Show yourself that you can challenge or twist the neural maps in your head rather than following the same synapses on the same daily journey. When you see the alterations that result from making unique choices and displaying unfamiliar behavior, the freshness is empowering.

It is a profound joy to make a new choice, complete a half-written sentence, stop mindlessly treading the same ruts you have already worn down.

An example came to me while gently rocking my two-year-old daughter in the dark. My "rutted" thinking was: "Please go to sleep quickly so I can watch *Ant-Man* with your thirteen-year-old brother. I'm tired, and I want what I want. . . ." My fresh thought was: "Just rock her and show her that this is who Dad is, that you are safe with Dad, that there is nowhere Dad would rather be but here, feeling your embrace."

This small example is exactly the point. Start small. Build confidence through practice. Breaking through old walls or bursting out of our myriad ruts is feasible with effort, sincerity, and conviction. We must understand that we can double down in any moment of life to increased empathy, wider perspective, deeper love, fuller spirit. We must also become more disciplined if we want a new map written in our head, one we can behold with beauty.

Make a list of the changes in thinking and behavior you want or need to make.

♦ ♦ ♦

QUESTIONS/EXERCISES

What changes to my thinking do I want?
_____
_____
_____
_____

What changes to my behavior do I want?
_____
_____
_____
_____
_____

What changes to my beliefs do I want?
_____
_____
_____
_____
_____

PERCEPTION

"We can't solve problems by using the same kind of thinking we used when we created them."
—Albert Einstein

When on a dark winter evening in 2011 I returned from my four-hour roundtrip commute from Manhattan and entered my parents' home, I was relieved to learn that a dinner plate was waiting for me in the oven. Staying in my parents' basement for a year after selling our starter home and saving for a bigger house for my wife and two young sons, we had settled into the strange routine of being guests in my childhood home.

I reached into the oven and withdrew a Saran-wrapped plate and made my way to a seat. About fifteen seconds later, I suddenly had the sensation that the plate was warm.

That was all. But over the next six days my right index finger became swollen and aggravated, causing increasingly more painful pulses, especially in the night. It disturbed me enough to go to the ER.

After examining the finger, the doctor said, "I don't know how you have been dealing with this pain. You have a severe internal burn. Whatever you touched or grabbed was hot enough to liquefy much of the fat in your finger. I don't know how you were able to hold onto the plate for so long. You must be really tough."

But I was not tough at all. At the time, had I more courage and honesty, I would have explained to him that 150mg of Oxycodone a day would make Tinkerbell that tough.

Had I really been tough I would not have become so frightened of life that I had to immerse my consciousness in opiates to make life manageable. Nevertheless, this experience makes an important point about perception. My senses told me the plate was cool and safe. Perceptions can be wrong. Even our best sober perceptions can give us dangerously wrong or insufficient data about the world. It may be that the brain is more reliable when we're sober, but when we're on drugs, I have much less confidence in our thinking and awareness.

Perception plays a significant role in human dysfunction. Our egos are remarkably adept at endlessly repeating behaviors that produce terrible outcomes. We ignore people and things that give us meaning and seek out things that offer us more wealth or stuff even when we have enough for survival. We push people away when we should let them in.

We respond with pride or defiance when allowing ourselves to be vulnerable is less harmful.

To approach our perceptions differently means we must become open to the flaws in our life: which behaviors are clearly failing, and which of our strategies should be renounced.

Our perception is intrinsically biased. While our perception can never be perfect, we must be willing to challenge our views of life and our problems. We must break the myopia we often suffer in our analysis of how to handle an interpersonal conflict or negative habit. Often, in moments of frustration, our default is to employ the skills we've learned from our parents or that have emerged from our past conflicts and insecurities. In other words, our perceptions are often, perhaps even mainly, flawed. In frustration or insecurity, we lose the connection to our prefrontal cortex, which is involved in judgment, and act on emotion and ingrained habit. We then pay the price some hours later when we calm down and must live with our behavior or a person we hurt.

> *"When the only tool you have is a hammer, you tend to see every problem as a nail."*
> –Abraham Maslow

Many of us employ our default reactions to bludgeon our loved ones in anger or withdraw and ice them out for days. Raging outbursts, passive aggressive attacks—these tools become our only weapon for defense. Many times, these extreme reactions were once an appropriate reaction for self-defense or survival. We developed them to manage an abusive parent or early trauma and don't realize we can discard them. It's like having only an axe in the toolshed. We can and need to collect other tools that are more appropriate and more effective in delivering what we want.

Many of our emotional reactions are like old, worn-out records, or like songs deep in our past that continue to impact the music we hear and create today. Recognize that you must commit to analyzing your reactions, report them to a therapist, a spouse, a spiritual adviser, or a trusted friend to account for them and receive feedback to help you widen your perception.

Being able to see and consider your behavior from multiple viewpoints is to loosen the hold that perception and unconscious behavior have over you. Revisit your view of reality through others' eyes and their perceptions to get closer to your truth. Never do I feel shallower in my grasp on reality than when I click into an opposite point of view, one that illuminates the imbalance of how I was looking at something. This happens more often than I would like. Reforming our perception involves a disciplined caution in making the leap between "my" perception and reality.

This is a good starting point to shake up our certainty vis-à-vis our viewpoint and seek an open mind and fresh perceptions. We are continuously renegotiating our relationship with reality. Some might say that the accuracy with which we do this corelates directly to how effectively and fully we can live.

Consistently "remapping" our life, much as how a bat verifies its surroundings by echolocation, improves our ability to view life truthfully. Becoming more closely aligned with what is real is immensely helpful in avoiding what is not real. Seeing which of our fears or perceptions are not real frees up immense resources to more skillfully handle our actual issues. I think it is wise to remind oneself every morning that there is *the* reality and then there is *my* reality.

It is helpful to start a new day remembering that we possess only one narrow window into the divine and we must assume that there is always more than we are seeing. There are billions of other windows that display a view of reality equally true. Look for assistance through your spirituality and through other people to stay grounded and open to finding the truth.

Even when we are grounded, being triggered by rude or threatening behavior can hijack our emotions When this occurs, we may zoom into our narrow worldview and lose sight of other ways to interpret the situation. We are flooded with emotions—fear, anger, disgust, defensiveness. We lash out or otherwise lose access to our rationality and perspective.

Our optic nerves transmit the visual data we see to the brain. The moment this occurs, our brains light up, tracking our many associations and emotions and figuring out how an image makes us feel.

When this occurs and your brain classifies something as frightening, emotionally dangerous, obnoxious or unpleasant, practice taking those labels with a grain of salt. Remind yourself that the data you're seeing is neither perfect nor necessarily accurate. It is a judgment you're making on what your memories and experience decide that data means.

Your initial assessment is critical. When the first link in the chain of a human interaction is misread, it can easily develop into an avalanche of miscommunication and tension. If you are frightened and irritated, you are likely to misperceive others' behavior, language, and movements. Being mindful of your perception when you are emotionally troubled helps you guard against quick reactions or overreactions.

Treat your perceptions with curiosity and sensitivity. Put them in the "possible" category before you load the wrong reaction into the chamber and "fire" at the person nearest you. Taking a little longer to come to an accurate judgment is far better than reacting inappropriately. Do you believe you have a negative, cynical, or pessimistic view of the world or human beings? How do you view the world right now? Being honest about this will help you examine your misperceptions.

Generalized perception happens constantly. For example, when we decide that a person who cut us off in traffic is selfish and assume they think their time is more important than ours. We accept and give life to that story, which can dominate our mind for minutes—or an entire afternoon or night. That souring in our mood can easily snowball into tension, conflict, and stress.

That first negative or destructive perception is a domino that has the power to set off a chain reaction of unhappiness.

Someone with a more positive perception of people could as easily perceive something different, such as: "Wow, that was scary. That person is in such a rush. They must have an emergency. Maybe their wife is in labor? Maybe they're late for an interview?"

It's not about praising positive people and knocking those with negative perceptions. It's about the power of your worldview to affect *everything* in your life. If we want to write a new chapter for ourselves, we must examine our biases and be willing to rip up the old stories in our head. Believing that we can create and control a new story, we can set out with renewed vigilance toward what we conclude about people's words and actions.

Someone once said, "You are only as big as the smallest thing that gets you angry." If we can agree that when we are unstable, our perception is likely to be negative, we realize that allowing small things to destabilize us is significant.

What are the smallest things that make you mad? Can you work toward becoming less triggered or activated by peoples' comments and behavior? To have more control you must take it, recognizing the futility of allowing your emotional state to be determined by others. Will your emotional state always be affected by others? Probably, yes, as it should be when we are in caring and deep relationships.

But if we allow others' actions to dictate or unhinge our wellbeing we must use practice and discipline to create distance between their behaviors and our reactions. We must stop the triggers, sometimes one at a time, that lead old perceptions to unhealthy reactions and dysfunctional results.

All this is theory unless we commit to questioning our entire perceptual map of the world. Taking steps to stabilize your nervous system through meditation, exercise, prayer, diet, and having sufficient emotional support will lay the groundwork for perceiving in a more positive way.

Once this maintenance is achieved you can begin perceiving differently, more positively, and see new and unique possibilities emerge. Nothing is more empowering than observing a perception, watching yourself identify that there is a choice between an old, negative view and a fresh perspective, and the experience of adopting the new, healthier view. Just see yourself do that a few times.

Identifying choices in labeling and characterizing perceptions is like discovering magic. As you introduce this power more choices will appear and previously unseen routes and unanticipated behaviors will manifest. The timeframe we have to influence a thought or perception will lengthen, as will the fuse on the bomb of skewed perceptions. We will experience a growing ability to easily extinguish the bomb if we so choose. This can save you a million apologies and a billion bad moods. If you can slow down your perception and discern more thoughtfully, you can pick the kinds of behavior that keep you from lashing out, losing self-control, and saying or doing things you feel ashamed of. You can and should protect your emotional stability.

To create something new in your life you must single-mindedly staff the control room of your perceptions and "decide" what the output from the world means for your life. Perception is like a shadow on the surface of the water. Every one of us sees it differently.

"Decide" what it is you want to see. If you are looking for the negative you will find it in abundance. If you are looking for light and good, you will also find that in abundance. What will you look for now? If we are honest, we can admit that we have found what we are looking for. If we now want to "see" differently we must fire our imagination and faith to help us create new visions—ones worth looking for.

The visions I pursued in my life led me here. I viewed the world with fear and lived in misery as a result. I found all manner of frightening things—because I perceived things as frightening. Sometimes we identify emotionally dysfunctional "factory settings" later in life and gain delayed insight into how they have caused us trouble.

Perhaps the narrowness of our perception has limited our life until now. I urge you not to trade an old, narrow vision for a slightly larger vision. Let us invite in God, a higher power, nature, the universe—anything that allows us unlimited perception. Knock down the door to the room of perception. Should we not do that, we can become complacent, misguided, and stuck in narrow perspectives.

Focus on the limitlessness of life and creation. Embrace humility in acknowledging how little we know and become hospitable to new beliefs and ideas. If our vision remains strong and our actions steadfast, better results will follow.

Stop painting your old, dysfunctional perceptual picture. Set the stage for a new, functional picture by courageously imagining better. Imagine what your life can be with the energy and love it deserves. Stop rushing through unfocused days while repeating old habits and squandering potential. Truly take the time to reset. This will not happen unless you make it your priority to begin a totally different portrait of your life.

On the next page, write some notes about what you would like to perceive in this world.

♦ ♦ ♦

QUESTIONS/EXERCISES

What do you want to perceive in this world now?
What do you want to see?

SPIRITUALITY

> *"You have to grow from the inside out. None can teach you, none can make you spiritual. There is no other teacher but your own soul."*
> —Swami Vivekananda

To MAKE A FRESH START or begin a new phase in our life, we must address spirituality and untangle it from religion. Millions of suffering people dismiss spirituality due to a disdain for or dismissal of organized religion.

> *"You are not a human being having a spiritual experience. You are a spiritual being having a human experience."*
> —Pierre Teilhard de Chardin

We happen to be on a giant rotating ball of rock and water traveling at about 67,000 miles per hour at the bottom of a deep gravity well, orbiting a ball of fire about 865,000 miles wide. On this great ball, there is nothing ordinary about waking up and "being." Many people are caught up in the materialistic production and consumption galvanizing humanity. We are concerned with where our bodies are going, how we look on social media, and our dramas at work or at home. The car we are driving, the apartment we are decorating, the party we are attending steal our attention and our energies.

The physical consumes almost everything we have. What about the spiritual? What about the spirit most of us will admit we have? What are its needs and how do we feed it?

Spirituality: the quality of being concerned with the human spirit or soul as opposed to material or physical things.

I am asking you to be concerned with your human spirit. Where is it? Take a minute for a deep breath and relaxation and see if you can feel it. If you do not feel it or are disconnected, when did you last feel it?

My spirit manifests to me in several ways. It feels like an endless well of light and grace. I see it in the eyes and hear it in the laughter of my children. It is an invitation to wade into that joyful well deep beneath the surface layers of thought and ego. These waves fill me with energy and strength. The Spirit is rooted in the concept of some power greater than yourself. In recovery we discuss the importance of believing in a higher power, something stronger than the drugs and alcohol, and even the self that has failed us.

Spirituality

The concept of a higher power was popularized through the New Thought movement of the nineteenth century. It argued that a supreme intelligence, or God, is everywhere. Alcoholics Anonymous made the term more widely known and it became an important part of all 12-step recovery programs. The concept flows out of the recognition we see when we realize we are in a cage we've built with our minds and can't find an exit alone. We reach a wall we cannot scale no matter how hard we try. The curse of Sisyphus pushing a boulder up a hill for eternity is a curse any addict, alcoholic, and many others can relate to.

We often find ourselves repeating the same dysfunctional loops of actions and thoughts due to the weight of habit. We stay stuck in the same ruts, but eventually, we must make a choice about faith. Where are you on the subject of belief? Many people in recovery use a 12-step group like Alcoholics Anonymous or Narcotics Anonymous as their higher power, or they use GOD (Group Of Drunks). But there is no need to believe anything to move toward spirituality.

Yet when we've exhausted our personal resources, examined our self-island endlessly and found it lacking, have shown ourselves the futility of making promises and pledges to stop drugs or alcohol, binge shopping or pushing people away, it is time to be open to new beliefs.

To learn about history's many mystics and prophets is to be tantalized with the possibilities for enlarging your perception and deepening your experience of this moment. For any change to occur we must become open at an entirely new level. We must seek to move from the physical to the spirit within us.

It is no small irony that one label for alcohol is spirits. "Spiritus" in Latin means breath, but it is unclear why alcohol became associated with the word. However, seeing how intoxicated people act, it is easy to guess. Many people become more animated, more jovial, more aggressive. Alcohol does indeed bring out a great deal of energy and emotion within people, with humorous or terrifying results. It brings out a projection of things deep within human beings.

I can understand why this might be associated with their "spirit." The irony is that this same substance has literally robbed many millions of their spirit. People have drowned their spirit in beer or vodka, schnapps or gin, crack or heroin.

Chemicals of abuse bring euphoric highs for some time, but they inevitably boomerang on any addict, darkening the spirit within as well as the person's outward behavior and functioning. Rather than freeing and strengthening the spirit, we give our priority to the liquid, the pill, or our limited and stuck ego. These chemicals, or circular neurotic thinking, keep us looking for an answer through our bodies' pleasure or our egos' grand plans.

If you have become lost in the hallway of depression, isolation, addiction, divorce, trauma, or loss of purpose, you need to embrace spirit. I want to ask you: what awakens your spirit?

Make a list of those things or people that light a spark inside you, something that fills you with joy and meaning. Even if that spark is tiny or that spirit is muffled and barely noticeable, let us awaken it into the fire you deserve.

QUESTIONS/EXERCISES

What awakens my spirit? (things, people, experiences that strengthen your connection to spirit)

_____
_____
_____
_____
_____
_____
_____
_____
_____
_____
_____
_____
_____
_____
_____
_____
_____
_____

What helps to engage our spirit is reaching out of ourselves and connecting with other forces. Look to the spirit of a god, of gods, of nature, of the universe, of a supreme intelligence, of a church, a temple, a group of people. Look for it by engaging your inner spirit with people and practices that stimulate and inspire you.

It is a funny thing that while our spirit is ours, we activate it most when engaging with the world and people in ways that are true to us and congruent with our beliefs. As we become conscious and connected to our spirit, we more clearly see the links between us and others, as well as our conception of a higher power in whatever form. When you come to believe more strongly in your spirit, it is impossible to ignore the spirits of others and the feeling that yours is linked with theirs.

The glory of spirituality is finally resting your feet upon something unmovable. After a lifetime of uncertainty with the ground shifting beneath the life you are trying to build, spirituality offers a connection to a footing that never has to move. Spirit, some thing or deity or service that provides your connection to the ultimate reality, offers security and a handle to hold onto while the material world continues its chaos.

That is the key. That despite the chaos of our surroundings, the unpredictability of human beings, the impermanence of our possessions, there can be something permanent: a room you carry deep inside you. First, come to believe the spirit is in that room, and then be willing to invite that power into your life.

Spirituality

Many of us don't come to believe in spirit until life has knocked us around sufficiently. Through the jostling and the knocks we take, somehow, a crack appears, and the delusion of a life lived solely on self-sufficiency gets shattered. It is said that religion is for people who don't want to go to hell, and spirituality is for people who have already been there.

I like to visualize spirituality as a well that has no bottom. I feel it throughout my days and nights. In difficult times I welcome those waters to refresh and replenish my spirit. At any moment I can close my eyes and feel its presence and its invitation to join with it. Spirit has strengthened me and lifted me above my many defects and shortcomings to be of more use to my brothers and sisters.

I implore all of you working on a reset or a new life to open your mind and your heart to the unlimited power of spirituality to help you get there.

On the next page, please list some actions to begin the exploration of your spiritual life: prayer, meditation, groups, church, bible study, recovery meetings, self-help meetings, retreats, daily readings, etc.

❖ ❖ ❖

QUESTIONS/EXERCISES

To deepen my spirituality I will . . .

SERVICE

"The end of all knowledge should be service to others."
—Cesar Chavez

In 1181, Francesco di Pietro di Bernardone was born in Assisi, Italy, to a prosperous Italian merchant and his wife. He enjoyed a pleasant and full life as a young man, learning Latin and displaying a great joy for living. After fighting in a war between the provinces Assisi and Perugia in 1202, Francis was captured and held as a prisoner of war for one year. After his release, while recovering from a serious illness, he became convinced that he should join the priesthood. He reportedly experienced visions or dreams that guided him toward God. Prior to renouncing his belongings, including his rich clothing, he is reported to have said: *"This is what I wish; this is what I am seeking. This is what I want to do from the bottom of my heart."*

From that point on, Francis's service to the people of Italy became legendary. He made a vow to serve and care for the poor. He discovered and passed along in his famous prayer that "It is by self-forgetting that one finds." Some 841 years later, St. Francis remains a beacon to millions of people in displaying the treasure of service and the self-liberation that accompanies selfless acts. He also sent a powerful message to all of us sinners who think we are unworthy.

"God could not have chosen anyone less qualified, or more of a sinner, than myself. And so, for this wonderful work He intends to perform through us, He selected me—for God always chooses the weak and the absurd, and those who count for nothing." St. Francis of Assisi

When we think of such figures as unreachable saints who don't seem human we do ourselves and them a great disservice. It is remarkable how many saints or prophets experienced their share of sin, war, and temptations before hitting their own rock bottoms. We must see them as human if we are to open a similar portal of transformation in our lives. We must understand how their example of the gift of service offers us untold riches and avenues to increased freedom of the human spirit.

What does it mean to serve others? Is it a stretch to say we would live in a far better world if we all focused more on serving others? People throughout history and today have displayed the joys and rewards of service. Is there something else of value in the world if we are not serving each other?

To see that your behavior helps people in crucial ways is a beautiful thing. For example, we can support people without food or housing, or those with mental illness and addiction issues. We can support the disabled or the elderly or the ill and the despairing. We can support trans or LGBTQ youth. We can help people who've been laid low to regain the strength to get back on their feet.

The power of lending others strength is one of the greatest discoveries I've ever made. It was strong magic in helping me get off the ground and restart my life. For those wishing to start over, service is a powerful tool. Perhaps you already serve well through your current job. Many people serve society through their work and contributions. You might volunteer time through a church, a shelter, or a nonprofit.

I often speak with individuals who feel bored, depressed, or lack purpose in their lives. They are struggling. Life is not terrible, but it's just not "enough." It feels grey, monotone, complacent. I frequently recommend that they get involved in service.

For the last 4 months I have been sitting with my hospice client James. A 92 year old Korean war vet with dementia and cancer, James can be very challenging to understand. Yet that is the gift he has given me. He reminded me of the power of authentic presence and loving touch. He reaches out to shake hands and squeezes my hand to connect. We nod our heads together to remind us that the human bond is beyond words. This is the invitation to humanity service gives us if we follow it.

Do you want to feel more purpose in your life? Escort sick and elderly people at a local hospital. See the look on a homeless child's face when you give her a new toy. Find joy in sitting with an older man in a nursing home who has no one to visit him. Serve trays of steaming vegetables at a soup kitchen and watch people who are without resources feel taken care of and supported.

With the unlimited treasures available through service, it is a shame that many of us don't do more. If you want to feel gratitude for how much you have, bend down and help those with significantly less. When you meet a woman living in a tent, you will realize that your house is a palace. You will gain perspective on the size of your own mental discomfort when you hear from the active schizophrenic at war with multiple voices or a bipolar individual whose depressive episodes confine them to bed for weeks. You will regain your spirit and positive attitude when you hear someone with harder circumstances and fewer resources who is fighting with twice your energy and showing the power of the human spirit.

You don't earn these realizations by eating donuts on your couch or going home from work every night to watch the same TV shows and think the same negative or limiting thoughts about your life.

> *"I am the pipe, not the well. This power flows through me, not from me."*
> —Recovery Speaker

Service takes a million forms, and we are responsible for searching and being both creative and persistent in our search for the form of service that will bring us deeper into life. It is out there. For most of my life I lived as if I was the well—that I was all I needed. But I was a disconnected entity. As the beginning of this story lays out, that life of disconnection almost killed me.

I believe starting over in any form involves discovering how we can connect to greater sources of power. How we can position ourselves in attitude, belief, and actions to relate more with other people and our spirituality. It is validating to be part of something bigger than yourself or to rejoin humanity with more depth and meaning.

Be on the lookout for how you can become the pipe—a more integrated piece of the universe, rather than a lonely well. Stagnant waters quickly spoil. We must find what moves our energy into the world and fills us with fresh resources. A counselor in rehab once held up a bottle of water. Holding his hand at the top, he stated, "You can only give away the excess, you must not empty out your reservoir on other people. You have to take in enough to replenish what you gave."

The three major crashes I suffered in my life resulted from giving more to people than I could maintain. I did not take in enough to replenish my well, because my faucet was turned on full blast. Take a lesson from that. You must value yourself enough to refill your own spiritual and mental energy.

Service may be our strongest and most dependable tool to lift that cover that keeps us closed in. If you want something different than what you have, put yourself in the environment of service and lift the floodgate. You cannot know or imagine the grace that will emerge from you letting yourself be the pipe.

I can promise you from my experience that you'll receive more than you imagined possible. Grounding and restoring your priorities and perspective is a magic you cannot create behind the walls of your own mind.

◆ ◆ ◆

QUESTIONS/EXERCISES

How are you serving others—even in small ways?

_____
_____

How could you serve others if you
gave more time and energy?

_____
_____

What do you hope to find in service?

_____
_____

Do some research and write down the
best options you can find to serve.

_____
_____
_____
_____
_____

QUESTIONS ASKED THROUGHOUT THE BOOK:

1. What is the obstacle standing in your way?

2. What do you want a second act of your life to look like?

3. What mental or physical limits are in your way?

4. What gains do you want on your mental health?

5. What changes do you want to your thinking?

6. What changes do you want to your perception?

7. How can you best be of service to others?

CONCLUSION

"What you seek is seeking you."
—Jalaluddin Rūmī

If you are reading this, I hope this last section truly marks the beginning of a better path in your journey through life. Let it be one marked by freshness in thought and action, in word and in imagination.

Be conscious from this moment forward of the need to focus all your energy on seeking correct perception and action. Be conscious of the lesson you must take from the obstacle currently standing before you.

Don't repeat the same loop. If you have looked to the wrong person for love again and again, looked for satisfaction in the wrong type of job or role, or trapped yourself from transforming into a better version of yourself, it's time to make the change.

Try the new thing. Explore the dream or hobby you have ignored or dismissed. Look for someone who will give you respect and love. Seek people and resources that get you off your island of self and place you back into a higher form of living. It is not our purpose on this planet to spend all our time and energy on producing enough stuff for our families and ourselves to get by.

If we are not extremely intentional, our lives can feel like a grinding race from cradle to grave, one focused out of necessity on chasing down jobs and raises to ensure we earn enough for a comfortable life.

Hopefully, this book can be a small nudge to slow down, reset, and find the spirit within you again. Spirit can be accessed, celebrated, and used to transform your experience of each day. At any time, we can intensify our support for the spirit within and bolster our actions to access it. Accept that you cannot be one with spirit making excuses not to push yourself and mindlessly scrolling through your YouTube and Instagram feeds endlessly.

Seek to sharpen your motivation daily. All it takes is a few days of complacency or rationalization for that motivation to rust over and become ineffective. Most importantly, focus on the vision you are gaining for the kind of life you want. Continue allocating time and energy to infuse that vision with power and clarity. Connect with it each morning and check on it throughout the day.

People are like asteroid tails. An asteroid passing through our solar system emits a long tail of gas and debris. It shows us where it has been, where it is going, and what it is dragging behind it. As humans, we too are passing through this universe and displaying our baggage in our wake. To really see a person is to see their past's effect on the present and the direction of their future. We must increase awareness of our "tail" and where our past is aiming us.

We all need a heading to set the sail toward, and based on our past experiences, we need to check those coordinates regularly. Involving spirituality in that coordinate setting is critical. How many times have we fallen into the same hole or navigated ourselves back onto the same rocks? Involve faith and outside accountability in your destination, rather than solely trusting your mind as the explorer it pretends to be.

After all, your real destination is to delve deeper within yourself. As you begin a second act in your life, you'll likely develop all manner of different behaviors and external consequences, but the real measure is feeling more integrity within and more peace in your interactions with the world. The motivational speaker Myles Munroe once said: "The wealthiest place in the world is not the gold mines of South America or the oil fields of Iraq and Iran. They are not the diamond mines of South Africa or the banks of the world. The wealthiest place on the planet is just down the road. It is the cemetery. There lie buried companies that were never started, inventions that were never made, bestselling books that were never written, and masterpieces that were never painted. In the cemetery is buried the greatest treasure of untapped potential."

I beg you not to be part of that great tragedy of unfulfilled achievements, untaken actions, and untested dreams.

There's nothing worse than a dream never realized, one that follows you into the ground like a neglected, dried seed. If we listed those people who have fought through darkness and doubt to fulfill what is within them, I believe the list would be too short. Please make sure you are on it. Start Act Two now and give it everything within you. Do so, and you will be continually amazed at how much more was within you all along. There will be no more room for doubt.

May you find grace, liberation, and belonging on your journey.

www.ingramcontent.com/pod-product-compliance
Lightning Source LLC
Chambersburg PA
CBHW042012060526
44119CB00123B/435/J